Reading/Writing Companion

129235

+11,9102

Mc
Graw
Hill

mheducation.com/prek-12

Send all inquiries to:
McGraw Hill
1325 Avenue of the Americas
New York, NY 10019

ISBN: 978-1-26-575799-1
MHID: 1-26-575799-2

Printed in the United States of America.

3 4 5 6 7 8 9 LMN 26 25 24 23 22   B

Welcome to WONDERS!

We're here to help you set goals to build on the amazing things you already know. We'll also help you reflect on everything you'll learn.

Let's start by taking a look at the incredible things you'll do this year.

You'll build knowledge on exciting topics and find answers to interesting questions.

You'll read fascinating fiction, informational texts, and poetry and respond to what you read with your own thoughts and ideas.

And you'll research and write stories, poems, and essays of your own!

Here's a sneak peek at how you'll do it all.

"Let's go!"

You'll explore new ideas by reading groups of different texts about the same topic. These groups of texts are called *text sets*.

At the beginning of a text set, we'll help you set goals on the My Goals page. You'll see a bar with four boxes beneath each goal. Think about what you already know to fill in the bar. Here's an example.

I can read and understand expository text.

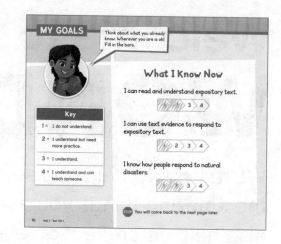

As you move through a text set, you'll explore an essential question and build your knowledge of a topic until you're ready to write about it yourself.

You'll also learn skills that will help you reach your text set goals. At the end of lessons, you'll see a new Check In bar with four boxes.

CHECK IN 1 2 3 4

Reflect on how well you understood a lesson to fill in the bar.

Here are some questions you can ask yourself.

- Was I able to complete the task?

- Was it easy, or was it hard?

- Do I think I need more practice?

You have plenty of tools and resources to learn more, such as anchor charts and center activities. You can also reread a lesson or ask a teacher or peer for help.

It's okay if I think I need more practice. The most important thing is that I do my best and keep learning!

Thinking about what works best for me will help me choose what to do next.

At the end of each text set, you'll show off the knowledge you built by completing a fun task. Then you'll return to the second My Goals page where we'll help you reflect on all that you learned.

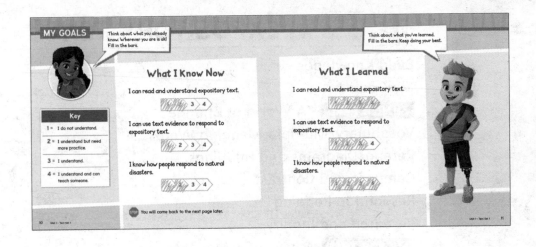

I'll fill in a new set of bars to show how far I've come. I started at 2, but now I'm at 4 because I can read and understand an expository text well enough to teach a friend.

I'll follow the same steps as I write my own stories, essays, and poems. I own my learning, and you can own yours!

"Let's get started!"

TEXT SET 1 **EXPOSITORY TEXT**

Build Knowledge 8

My Goals 10

SHARED READ "A World of Change" 12

Vocabulary/Multiple-Meaning Words 16

Reread/Diagrams and Headings 18

Compare and Contrast 20

Respond to Reading 22

Research and Inquiry 23

ANCHOR TEXT Analyze *Earthquakes* 24

Respond to Reading 27

PAIRED SELECTION Analyze "Weathering the Storm" 28

Author's Craft: Author's Perspective 31

Make Connections/Show Your Knowledge 32

TEXT SET 2 **REALISTIC FICTION**

Build Knowledge 34

My Goals 36

SHARED READ "The Talent Show" 38

Vocabulary/Idioms 42

Make Predictions/Plot 44

Plot: Conflict 46

Respond to Reading 48

Research and Inquiry 49

ANCHOR TEXT Analyze *Experts, Incorporated* 50

Respond to Reading 53

PAIRED SELECTION Analyze "Speaking Out to Stop Bullying" 54

Author's Craft: Author's Claim 57

Make Connections/Show Your Knowledge 58

TEXT SET 3 **ARGUMENTATIVE TEXT**

Build Knowledge 60

My Goals 62

SHARED READ TIME *KiDS* "Dollars and Sense" 64

Vocabulary/Suffixes 68

Reread/Graphs and Headings 70

Central Idea and Relevant Details 72

Respond to Reading 74

Research and Inquiry 75

ANCHOR TEXT Analyze *Kids in Business* 76

Respond to Reading 78

PAIRED SELECTION Analyze "Starting a Successful Business" ... 79

Author's Craft: Sequence 81

Make Connections/Show Your Knowledge 82

EXTENDED WRITING

My Goals 84

PROJECT 1 Argumentative Essay 86

PROJECT 2 Argumentative Essay 98

CONNECT AND REFLECT

SCIENCE "Landforms Shaped by Weathering and Erosion" 110

SCIENCE "Dust Bowl Blues" 111

Activities 113

SOCIAL STUDIES "Developing a Nation's Economy" 116

Activities 119

Reflect on Your Learning 121

Digital Tools

Find this eBook and other resources at **my.mheducation.com**

Kwaku Alston/Stockland Martel

5

TEXT SET 1 **EXPOSITORY TEXT**

Build Knowledge 122

My Goals 124

SHARED READ "Animal Adaptations" 126

Vocabulary/Prefixes 130

Summarize/Photographs, Captions, and Headings 132

Central Idea and Relevant Details 134

Respond to Reading 136

Research and Inquiry 137

ANCHOR TEXT Analyze *Spiders* 138

Respond to Reading 141

PAIRED SELECTION Analyze "Anansi and the Birds" 142

Author's Craft: Character Development 145

Make Connections/Show Your Knowledge 146

TEXT SET 2 **DRAMA**

Build Knowledge 148

My Goals 150

SHARED READ "The Ant and the Grasshopper" 152

Vocabulary/Antonyms 156

Ask and Answer Questions/Elements of a Play 158

Theme 160

Respond to Reading 162

Research and Inquiry 163

ANCHOR TEXT Analyze *Ranita, The Frog Princess* 164

Respond to Reading 167

PAIRED SELECTION Analyze "Pecos Bill and the Bear Lake Monster" 168

Author's Craft: Hyperbole 171

Make Connections/Show Your Knowledge 172

TEXT SET 3 **POETRY**

Build Knowledge 174

My Goals 176

SHARED READ "Dog" 178

Vocabulary/Similes and Metaphors 182

Rhyme and Structure/Lyric Poetry and Haiku 184

Character Perspective 186

Respond to Reading 188

Research and Inquiry 189

ANCHOR TEXT Analyze "Bat" 190

Respond to Reading 192

PAIRED SELECTION Analyze "Fog" 193

Author's Craft: Imagery and Assonance 195

Make Connections/Show Your Knowledge 196

EXTENDED WRITING

My Goals 198

PROJECT 1 Expository Essay 200

PROJECT 2 Expository Essay 212

CONNECT AND REFLECT

SCIENCE "Everglades Mammals" 224

SCIENCE "Nine-Banded Armadillos" 225

Activities 227

SOCIAL STUDIES "Volunteering at National Parks" 230

SOCIAL STUDIES "A Hero of Conservation" 231

Activities 233

Reflect on Your Learning 235

Writing Rubrics 236

 Digital Tools

Find this eBook and
other resources at
my.mheducation.com

Build Vocabulary

Write new words you learned about how people respond to natural disasters. Draw lines and circles for the words you write.

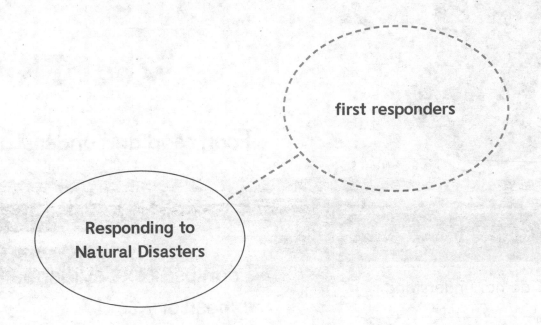

first responders

Responding to Natural Disasters

Go online to **my.mheducation.com** and read the "Masters of Disasters" Blast. What do you think is the most important characteristic of a first responder? Then blast back your response.

Masterfile

Think about what you already know. Wherever you are is okay. Fill in the bars.

Key

1 = I do not understand.

2 = I understand but need more practice.

3 = I understand.

4 = I understand and can teach someone.

What I Know Now

I can read and understand expository text.

1 2 3 4

I can use text evidence to respond to expository text.

1 2 3 4

I know how people respond to natural disasters.

1 2 3 4

 You will come back to the next page later.

Think about what you've learned.
Fill in the bars. Keep doing your best.

What I Learned

I can read and understand expository text.

1 2 3 4

I can use text evidence to respond to expository text.

1 2 3 4

I know how people respond to natural disasters.

1 2 3 4

My Goal I can read and understand expository text.

TAKE NOTES

As you read, make note of interesting words and important information.

A World of CHANGE

The Grand Canyon Skywalk in Arizona

Essential Question

?

How do people respond to natural disasters?

Read about how people prepare for natural disasters.

Earth may seem as if it is a large rock that never changes. Actually, our planet is in a constant state of change. Natural changes take place every day. These activities **alter** the surface of Earth. Some of these changes take place slowly over many years. Others happen in just minutes. Whether they are slow or fast, both kinds of changes have a great effect on our planet.

Slow and Steady

Some of Earth's biggest changes can't be seen. That is because they are happening very slowly. Weathering, erosion, and deposition are three natural processes that change the surface of the world. They do it one grain of sand at a time.

Weathering occurs when rain, snow, sun, and wind break down rocks into smaller pieces. These tiny pieces of rock turn into soil, but they are not carried away from the landform.

Erosion occurs when weathered pieces of rock are carried away by a natural force such as a river. This causes landforms on Earth to get smaller. They may even completely **collapse** over time. The Grand Canyon is an example of the effect of erosion. It was carved over thousands of years by the Colorado River.

After the process of erosion, dirt and rocks are then dropped in a new location. This process is called deposition. Over time, a large collection of deposits may occur in one place. Deposition by water can build up a beach. Deposition by wind can create a **substantial** landform, such as a sand dune.

FIND TEXT EVIDENCE

Read *I can*

Paragraph 1

Compare and Contrast

Underline the words that tell how some natural changes are different from other natural changes.

Paragraphs 2–5

Reread

Circle the three natural processes that slowly change Earth's surface.

Draw a box around the words that explain how the Grand Canyon was formed. What happens to dirt and rocks after the process of erosion? Write it here.

_____

_____

_____

Reread

Author's Craft

How does the author show you the causes and effects of natural processes?

FIND TEXT EVIDENCE

Read

▼
Paragraphs 1–3
Compare and Contrast

Underline the three different ways people try to stop beach erosion. Write them here.

1 _____

2 _____

3 _____

Paragraphs 4–5
Reread

Draw a box around the text that explains why volcanic eruptions and landslides are called natural disasters. **Circle** words that explain how magma moves.

What can happen when an eruption occurs without warning?

_____

Reread

Author's Craft

How does the author use headings to give and organize information?

Although erosion is a slow process, it still creates problems for people. Some types of erosion are dangerous. They can be seen as a **hazard** to communities.

To help protect against beach erosion, people build structures that block ocean waves from the shore. They may also use heavy rocks to keep the land from eroding. Others grow plants along the shore. The roots of the plants help hold the soil and make it less likely to erode.

Unfortunately, people cannot protect the land when fast natural processes occur.

Fast and Powerful

Fast natural processes, like slow processes, change the surface of Earth. But fast processes are much more powerful. They are often called natural disasters because of the **destruction** they cause. Volcanic eruptions and landslides are just two examples.

Volcanoes form around openings in Earth's crust. When pressure builds under Earth's surface, hot melted rock called magma is forced upwards. It flows up through the volcano and out through the opening. Eruptions can occur without warning. They have the potential to cause a **crisis** in a community.

Like volcanic eruptions, landslides can happen without warning. They occur when rocks and dirt, loosened by heavy rains, <u>slide</u> down a hill or mountain. Some landslides are small. Others can be quite large and cause **severe** damage.

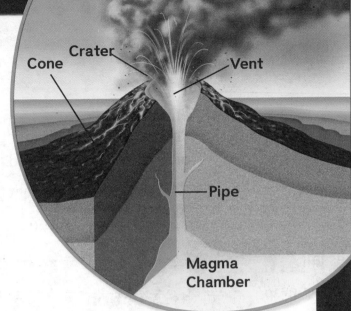

Cone
Crater
Vent
Pipe
Magma Chamber

Be Prepared

In contrast to slow-moving processes, people cannot prevent the effects of fast-moving natural disasters. Instead, scientists try to predict when these events will occur so that they can warn people. Still, some disasters are **unpredictable** and strike without warning. It is important for communities to have an emergency plan in place so that they can be evacuated quickly.

The surface of Earth constantly changes through natural processes. These processes can be gradual or swift. They help to make Earth the amazing planet that it is!

Summarize

Use your notes, the diagram, and the images to help you summarize "A World of Change." Compare slow and fast changes to Earth's surface.

EXPOSITORY TEXT

FIND TEXT EVIDENCE

Read

Paragraphs 1–3

Multiple-Meaning Words

In the second sentence in paragraph 1, the word *slide* is used as a verb. **Underline** context clues that help give the meaning. What is another meaning for *slide?*

_____

_____

Diagrams

Look at the diagram. How does the magma travel through the volcano? Write it here.

_____

_____

_____

_____

Reread

Author's Craft

What is the author's purpose for writing the section "Be Prepared"?

Vocabulary

Use the example sentences to talk with a partner about each word. Then answer the questions.

alter

The storm will **alter** the park if many trees fall.

What kinds of storms have you seen alter things in your state?

change

collapse

Floodwaters caused the bridge to **collapse**!

What might cause a tent to collapse?

To fall

crisis

Rescue workers help people during an emergency or **crisis**, such as a flood.

What other event might be a crisis?

emergency

destruction

The dogs ran through the store, causing a lot of damage and **destruction**.

How can wind cause destruction?

to break or destroy

hazard

That broken step is a **hazard** because someone might fall!

What else might be a hazard?

dangerous

Build Your Word List Pick one of the interesting words you noted on page 12 and look up its meaning. Then work with a partner to make a word web of synonyms, antonyms, and related words. Use a thesaurus to help you find words.

severe

Severe weather can include very strong winds and heavy rain.

What kinds of severe weather has your state had?

Bad

substantial

A **substantial** number of parents came to the meeting.

What is a synonym for *substantial*?

big / a lot

unpredictable

The **unpredictable** weather suddenly changed from sunny to rainy.

What is an antonym for *unpredictable*?

don't know whes

Multiple-Meaning Words

Some words may have more than one meaning. To figure out the meaning of a multiple-meaning word, check the words and phrases near it for clues.

🔍 FIND TEXT EVIDENCE

There are a few different meanings for the word block, *so it is a multiple-meaning word. The word* protect *and the phrase* "ocean waves from the shore" *help me figure out that the meaning for the word* block *in this sentence is* "stop."

To help protect against beach erosion, people build structures that block ocean waves from the shore.

Your Turn Use context clues to figure out the meanings of the following words in "A World of Change."

place, page 13, paragraph 1 _____

_____

shore, page 14, paragraph 2 _____

_____

CHECK IN 1 ⟩ 2 ⟩ 3 ⟩ 4 ⟩

Denis Jr. Tangney/Vetta/Getty Images

Reread

When you read an expository text, you may come across facts and ideas that are new to you. As you read "A World of Change," you can reread the difficult sections to make sure you understand them and to help you remember important details.

🔍 FIND TEXT EVIDENCE

You may not be sure why a volcano erupts. Reread the section "Fast and Powerful" on page 14 of "A World of Change."

> Page 14
>
> Volcanoes form around openings in Earth's crust. When pressure builds under Earth's surface, hot melted rock called magma is forced upwards. It flows up through the volcano and out through the opening. Eruptions can occur without warning. They have the potential to cause a **crisis** in a community.

I read that when pressure builds under Earth's surface, magma is forced upwards. From this I can draw the inference that pressure below the surface causes a volcano to erupt.

Your Turn What happens to rock during weathering? Reread the section "Slow and Steady" on page 13 to find out. As you read, remember to use the rereading strategy.

Rock is broken down into smaller pieces by sun rain snow and W

Quick Tip

If you read something you don't understand, stop and write or draw what you do not understand on a sticky note. Read the text again and look for context clues. Rereading may make the meaning clear. Use these sentence starters to help you.

- *I don't know . . .*
- *I reread that . . .*
- *Now I know that . . .*

Readers to Writers

An expository text tells readers about a topic. History lessons, science books, and biographies are examples of expository texts. The author presents a central idea and supports it with facts and evidence. The information in the text helps you to make inferences, or reach conclusions based on the evidence.

CHECK IN 1 > 2 > 3 > 4 >

Diagrams and Headings

The selection "A World of Change" is an expository text. Expository text gives facts, examples, and explanations about a topic. It may include text features—such as diagrams, headings, or charts—that organize information.

FIND TEXT EVIDENCE

"A World of Change" is an expository text. It gives many facts about Earth's processes. Each section has a heading that tells me what the section is about. The diagram gives me more information on the topic.

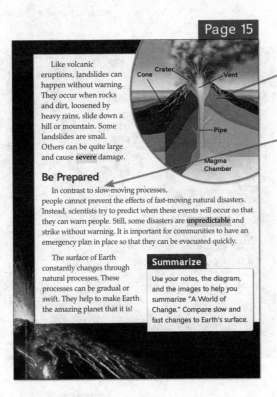

Page 15

Like volcanic eruptions, landslides can happen without warning. They occur when rocks and dirt, loosened by heavy rains, slide down a hill or mountain. Some landslides are small. Others can be quite large and cause **severe** damage.

Be Prepared

In contrast to slow-moving processes, people cannot prevent the effects of fast-moving natural disasters. Instead, scientists try to predict when these events will occur so that they can warn people. Still, some disasters are **unpredictable** and strike without warning. It is important for communities to have an emergency plan in place so that they can be evacuated quickly.

The surface of Earth constantly changes through natural processes. These processes can be gradual or swift. They help to make Earth the amazing planet that it is!

Summarize

Use your notes, the diagram, and the images to help you summarize "A World of Change." Compare slow and fast changes to Earth's surface.

Labels in diagram: Cone, Crater, Vent, Pipe, Magma Chamber

Diagrams Diagrams show the parts of something or the way a process works. They have labels for their different parts.

Headings Headings tell what a section of text is mostly about.

COLLABORATE

Your Turn List three text features in "A World of Change." Tell your partner what information you learned from each of the features.

_____

_____

_____

_____

CHECK IN 1 2 3 4

Compare and Contrast

Authors use text structure to organize the information in a text. Comparison is one kind of text structure. Authors who use this text structure tell how things are alike and different.

 FIND TEXT EVIDENCE

Looking back at pages 13–14 of "A World of Change," I can reread to learn how slow natural processes and fast natural processes are alike and different. Words such as some, but, both, *and* like *let me know that a comparison is being made.*

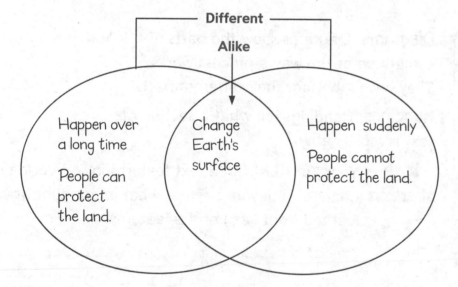

Different

Alike

Happen over a long time

People can protect the land.

Change Earth's surface

Happen suddenly

People cannot protect the land.

Your Turn Reread the section "Fast and Powerful" on pages 14–15. Compare and contrast volcanoes and landslides. List the information in the graphic organizer on page 21.

Westend61/Getty Images

CHECK IN 1 2 3 4

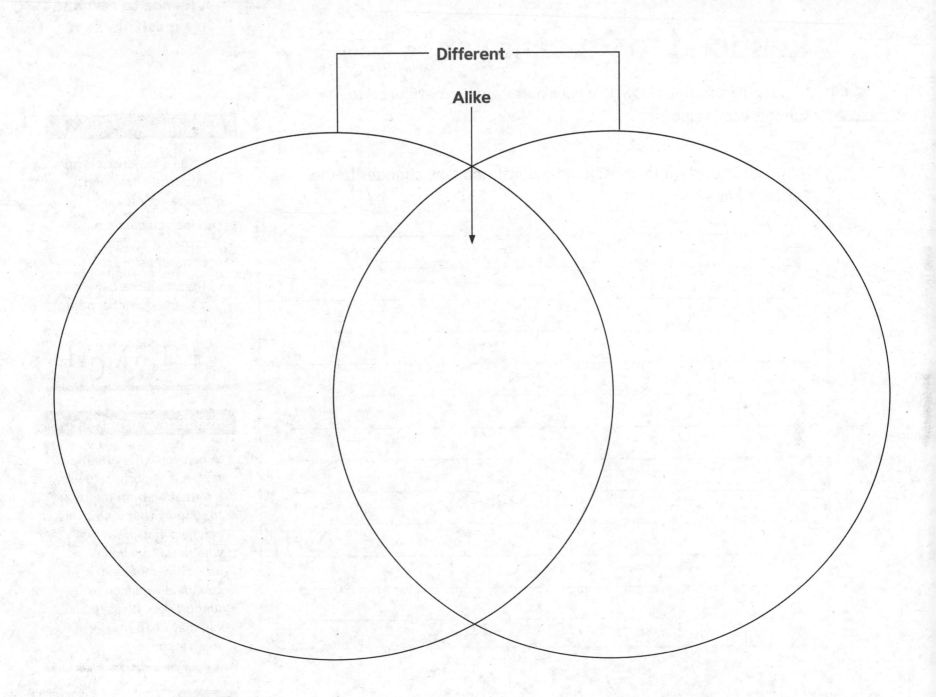

Different

Alike

Respond to Reading

Discuss the prompt below. Use your notes and text evidence to support your response.

> Why is it important to understand the fast and slow changes to the Earth's surface?
>
> _____
>
> _____
>
> _____
>
> _____
>
> _____
>
> _____
>
> _____
>
> _____
>
> _____
>
> _____
>
> _____
>
> _____

Quick Tip

Use these sentence starters to discuss the text and organize your ideas.

- *Understanding the causes of Earth's changes helps . . .*
- *The difference between fast and slow changes to the Earth's surface is . . .*
- *An example of a fast change is . . .*

Readers to Writers

When you write about a text, it is important to use information from that text to support your ideas. This can help you know whether or not you understand the text. If you can't find evidence to support your ideas, than you may need to revise your response.

CHECK IN 1 2 3 4

Natural Disasters

Knowing the best way to respond to a natural disaster can help keep people safe. Follow the research process to create a pamphlet that tells how to prepare for and be safe during one kind of natural disaster. Include scientific information telling what causes the disaster. Work with a partner.

Step 1 **Set a Goal** Brainstorm a list of natural disasters and choose one for your pamphlet. Then list questions you want your research to answer.

Step 2 **Identify Sources** Use books, magazines, websites, and videos to find information and images for your pamphlet.

Step 3 **Find and Record Information** Plagiarism is copying an author's words and ideas and using them as your own. As you take notes, avoid plagiarism by paraphrasing, or writing information in your own words. You also need to cite where your information came from and create a list of sources.

Step 4 **Organize and Synthesize Information** Analyze your information, including the images. Decide what information you want to use and how you will organize it. For example, do you want to use headings?

Step 5 **Create and Present** Create your pamphlet and decide how you will present it to the class.

> Still, some disasters are unpredictable and strike without warning. It is important for communities to have an emergency plan in place so that they can be evacuated quickly.

The excerpt above is from "A World of Change." Circle the text below that is a paraphrase of the excerpt.

Since some disasters can happen suddenly, communities need to have an emergency evacuation plan in place.

Some disasters are unpredictable and strike without warning, so it is important for communities to have an emergency plan in place. That way they can be evacuated quickly.

CHECK IN 1 2 3 4

Earthquakes

Literature Anthology: pages 10–19

? How does the author use photographs to help you understand what it is like to live through an earthquake?

Talk About It Reread **Literature Anthology** page 11 and look at the photograph. Talk to a partner about what you see in the photograph.

Cite Text Evidence How does the photograph help you understand what the text says? Use evidence from the text to explain how the photograph helps you better understand the text.

Photograph Clues	Text Evidence

Write The author uses a photograph to help me understand earthquakes by _____

_____

Synthesize Information

When you synthesize information, you make conclusions based on your own knowledge and new information you learn from a text. Combine what you already know about how Earth's surface changes during fast and slow natural processes. How do earthquakes and weathering each change the Earth's surface?

CHECK IN 〉 1 〉 2 〉 3 〉 4 〉

How is Dr. Cifuentes's account of the earthquake different from the information in the rest of the selection?

 Talk About It Reread **Literature Anthology** page 13. Turn to a partner and talk about how Dr. Cifuentes describes what it felt like to live through an earthquake.

Cite Text Evidence What words and phrases describe what happens during and after an earthquake? Use this chart to record text evidence.

Dr. Cifuentes's Description	What I Learned

Write Dr. Cifuentes's account helps me understand _____

_____

_____

CHECK IN 1 2 3 4

? How do you know that "Tsunami Terror" is a good heading for this section?

COLLABORATE

Talk About It Reread "Tsunami Terror" on pages 16–17 of the **Literature Anthology**. Turn to a partner and talk about how the author uses words to paint a picture of a tsunami.

Cite Text Evidence What words and phrases show that "Tsunami Terror" is a good heading for this section? Write text evidence in the web.

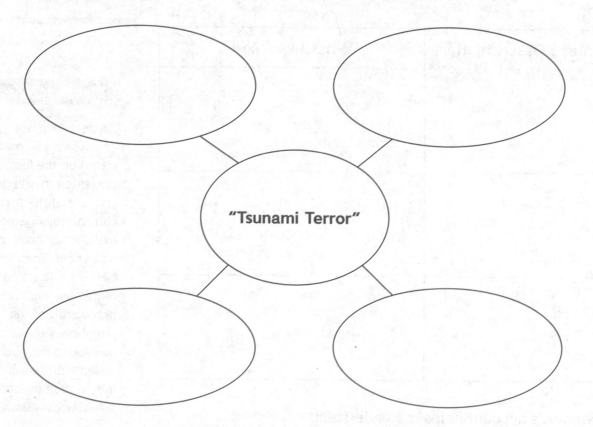

"Tsunami Terror"

Write "Tsunami Terror" is a good heading because _____

_____

CHECK IN 1 2 3 4

Respond to Reading

COLLABORATE

Discuss the prompt below. Use your notes and text evidence to support your response.

Why is it important to understand how earthquakes affect people?

_____

_____

_____

_____

_____

_____

_____

_____

_____

_____

_____

_____

_____

Quick Tip

Use these sentence starters to organize your text evidence.

- *One effect of an earthquake is . . .*
- *Understanding this effect helps . . .*
- *Another effect is . . .*
- *If you understand . . .*

CHECK IN 1 2 3 4

Weathering the Storm

Literature Anthology:
pages 22–23

[1]   I woke up at 5:00 a.m. to thunder and lightning. All morning it was pouring. All programs were canceled, which meant no horseback riding or tree climbing. Some of the troops had left that morning in case of flooding.

[2]   After lunch, I was walking to the bridge over the river. I looked at the field I had to cross and saw another river! Twenty-four hours earlier, the field had been dry. Our road was submerged, too. One thing was for sure: nobody was leaving our "island" anytime soon.

[3]   That night, a Brownie troop moved in with us. Their original cabin had been flooded through the chimney. There were tornado warnings that night, so to avoid more hazards, all of us kids piled into the bathroom to sleep.

Reread paragraph 2. **Draw a box** around the sentence that tells you a lot of rain fell in a short period of time.

Circle why the narrator says nobody was leaving the island anytime soon. Write the answer below.

_____

_____

_____

_____

COLLABORATE

Talk with a partner about how it is important for people to help each other during a natural disaster. **Underline** clues in paragraph 3 that tell how people helped each other.

4   When morning came, we were a little sore and tired, but we were all fine. The same could not be said for the road out! The water level was even higher than before. We hesitated to call the EMS because they were busy taking care of real emergencies. We had plenty of food, water, and board games, so we were not in crisis.

5   Some local troops left that day, taking the "emergency exit," an extremely muddy dirt road. But the problem of getting ourselves out remained. The main road was underwater, and the bridge would likely be ripped off by raging water. My mother's tiny car would never make it out on the muddy emergency exit road. We couldn't go on foot. We had to accept that we would have to stay another night and miss school and work.

Reread paragraph 4. **Underline** two reasons the Girl Scouts did not call EMS. Write the reasons in your own words here.

1_____

_____

_____

2_____

_____

_____

COLLABORATE

Look at the photograph and read the caption. Discuss why people may not be able to leave a flood area right away. **Circle** the sentences in paragraph 5 that tell why the narrator and others stayed another night.

The main road was underwater.

SPEED LIMIT 40

? How does the author order the events to help you understand what happens in a flood?

COLLABORATE

Talk About It Reread the excerpt on page 28. Talk with a partner about what happens at the camp.

Cite Text Evidence How does the author help you picture what a flood is and what it can do? Write text evidence in the chart.

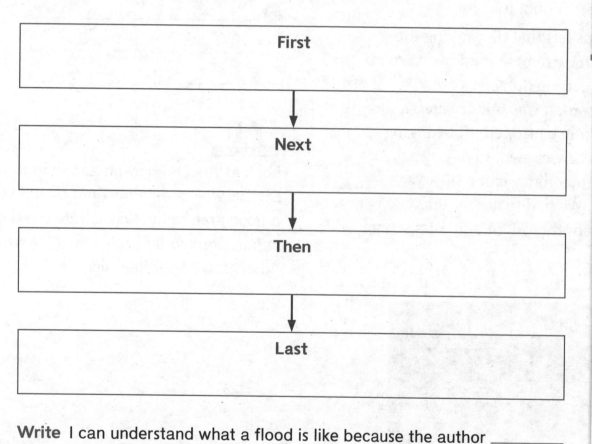

First

↓

Next

↓

Then

↓

Last

Write I can understand what a flood is like because the author _____

_____

_____

CHECK IN ⟩ 1 ⟩ 2 ⟩ 3 ⟩ 4 ⟩

Author's Perspective

An **author's perspective** is the attitude the author has toward a topic or subject. Authors don't always directly state their perspective toward something. Often they communicate their perspective by the information they choose to include and the language they use.

🔍 FIND TEXT EVIDENCE

In paragraph 4 on page 29 of "Weathering the Storm," the author describes how the storm affected her troop. They can't use the road out, but they are described as being "fine," having "plenty of food, water, and board games," and "not in crisis." These descriptions communicate the author's perspective that the storm wasn't so bad or frightening.

> . . .we were a little sore and tired, but we were all fine. The same could not be said for the road out! . . We hesitated to call the EMS because they were busy taking care of real emergencies. We had plenty of food, water, and board games, so we were not in crisis.

Your Turn Reread the last paragraph on page 23 of the **Literature Anthology**. What is the author's perspective on the trip? How do you know? _____

_____

_____

_____

Quick Tip

If an author's perspective isn't clearly stated, think about what the author chooses to tell and what he or she might not be telling. Do the words the author uses have a positive or negative feeling? How does the information affect the way you think about the subject?

CHECK IN 1 2 3 4

? **How does the photograph show how rescue workers respond after a natural disaster? How does it compare to what you read in _Earthquakes_ and "Weathering the Storm"?**

COLLABORATE

Talk About It Read the caption and look at the photograph. With a partner, talk about how the Coast Guard officer might feel about the devastation he sees from Hurricane Katrina. Talk about how you might feel.

Cite Text Evidence **Circle** clues in the photograph that show the effects of the hurricane. Then reread the caption and **underline** how technology helps people during natural disasters.

Write The photographer and the selections help me understand how people respond to a natural disaster by

_____

_____

_____

_____

_____

_____

U.S. Coast Guard photograph by Petty Officer 2nd Class NyxoLyno Cangemi

A Coast Guard officer rides in a Jayhawk helicopter over New Orleans on August 30, 2005, after Hurricane Katrina. Helicopters helped responders find and rescue people trapped on rooftops following the devastating hurricane.

CHECK IN 1 2 3 4

My Goal I know how people respond to natural disasters.

Create a Public Service Announcement

Think about what you learned about how natural disasters affect people and their communities. Create a public service announcement that tells why it's important to be prepared for natural disasters.

1 Look at your Build Knowledge notes in your reader's notebook.

2 Make a list of three things that are important to remember before and during a natural disaster. Use evidence from the texts you read to make your list. Tell why each one is important.

3 Write a script for your announcement. Try to include new vocabulary. Start with a hook to grab your listener's attention.

Think about what you learned in this text set. Fill in the bars on page 11.

Build Knowledge

Build Vocabulary

Write new words you learned about how your actions can affect others. Draw lines and circles for the words you write.

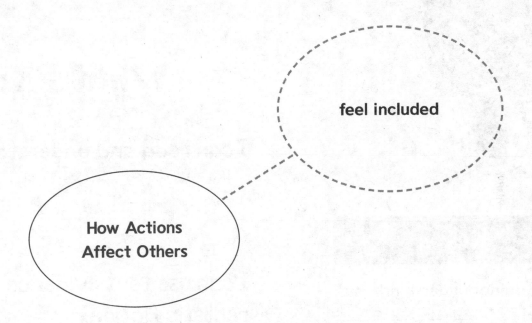

feel included

How Actions
Affect Others

Go online to **my.mheducation.com** and read the "Friends Forever" Blast. Think about the friendships you have read about in stories. What qualities does a good friend have? Then blast back your response.

Think about what you already know. Fill in the bars. There are no wrong answers here.

What I Know Now

I can read and understand realistic fiction.

| 1 | 2 | 3 | 4 |

Key

1 =	I do not understand.
2 =	I understand but need more practice.
3 =	I understand.
4 =	I understand and can teach someone.

I can use text evidence to respond to realistic fiction.

| 1 | 2 | 3 | 4 |

I know how my actions affect others.

| 1 | 2 | 3 | 4 |

 You will come back to the next page later.

Think about what you learned. Fill in the bars. What helped you the most?

What I Learned

I can read and understand realistic fiction.

1 2 3 4

I can use text evidence to respond to realistic fiction.

1 2 3 4

I know how my actions affect others.

1 2 3 4

My Goal I can read and understand realistic fiction.

TAKE NOTES

As you read, make note of interesting words and important details. _____

_____

_____

_____

_____

_____

_____

_____

_____

_____

_____

_____

_____

_____

THE Talent Show

Essential Question

How do your actions affect others?

Read about how Tina's actions affect Maura.

"Tina, there's a school talent show in three weeks," I shouted to my best friend. My older brother had been teaching me juggling, and I knew he'd help me with my act for the show.

Tina ran over to the bulletin board and read the poster. "Maura, what's our act going to be?" Tina asked me.

"Our act?" I said, taking a tighter grip on my books.

Tina grinned, pointed to the poster, and said, "It says acts can be individuals, partners, or small groups."

My grip on my books became **uncomfortably** tight. "You want to do an act together?"

"It'll be fun," Tina said.

I **hesitated** for a second before continuing. "I've got an idea and . . ."

Tina interrupted me. "Yeah, me too; let's talk at lunch."

During math, I tried to think of how I would tell Tina that I wanted to do my own act. After all, we are best friends; we should be able to see eye to eye about this. The problem is Tina always takes charge, I don't speak up, and then I end up feeling resentful about the whole situation.

I **desperately** wanted to win, but it was more than that. I wanted to win on my own—with an act that was all mine.

FIND TEXT EVIDENCE

Read

Paragraphs 1–8
Plot

Circle the dialogue that shows that Tina likes to take charge. Why is this information important to the story?

_____

_____

Paragraphs 9-10
Plot: Conflict

Underline the problem that Maura faces. What inference can you make about Maura?

_____

_____

_____

Reread
Author's Craft

How does the author's word choice help you predict how Maura might solve the problem?

FIND TEXT EVIDENCE

Read

Paragraphs 1–4

Idioms

Circle the words in paragraph 4 that help you understand the meaning of the idiom *to let off steam*.

Paragraphs 5–8

Make Predictions

What does Maura's grandmother say to encourage Maura to speak up for herself? **Draw a box** around the text evidence. Write what you predict will happen next.

_____

_____

_____

Reread

Author's Craft

How does the author use the character of Maura's grandmother to help Maura solve her problem?

At lunch, Tina started talking as soon as we sat down. "I have it all planned out. My **inspiration** came from that new TV show, *You've Got Talent*. We can sing along to a song and do a dance routine, and my mother can make us costumes."

"Yeah, that's good," I said. "But I had another idea." I told her about my juggling act.

Tina considered it. "Nah, I don't think I can learn to juggle in three weeks and I'd probably drop the balls," she said. "We don't want to be **humiliated**, right?"

At recess, I ran around the track a couple of times just to let off steam.

When my grandmother picked me up after school, she drove a few minutes and finally said, "Cat got your tongue?"

I explained about the talent show as she listened carefully. "So, Tina is not being respectful of your ideas, but it sounds as if you aren't either."

"What?" I shouted. "I told Tina her idea was good."

"No," said my grandmother, "I said that you weren't respectful of your own ideas, or you would have spoken up. I understand that you're friends, but you're still **accountable** for your own actions."

I thought about this. "So what should I do?" I asked.

"I **advise** you to tell the truth," she said. "It wouldn't hurt to let Tina know what you want. Besides," my grandmother added, "it will be good for your **self-esteem**!"

When we got home, I took 12 deep breaths, called Tina, and told her that I was going to do my juggling act. She was curt on the phone, and I spent all night worrying she would be mad at me.

The next day, she described her act and her costume. But the biggest surprise came at recess, when we played a game that I chose, not Tina.

I guess standing up for myself did pay off.

Summarize

Use your notes to summarize what happens in "The Talent Show."

FIND TEXT EVIDENCE 🔍

Read

Paragraphs 1-5

Plot: Conflict

Circle the dialogue that helps Maura think about how to solve her problem. What does Maura's grandmother want her to do?

_____

_____

Synthesize Information

How do Maura's actions affect Tina by the end of the story?

_____

_____

_____

_____

_____

Reread

Author's Craft

How does the author show how Maura feels after she stands up for herself?

Vocabulary

Use the example sentences to talk with a partner about each word. Then answer the questions.

accountable

Sami is held **accountable** when he forgets to walk his dog.

How are the words *accountable* and *responsible* similar?

When you are held accountable, you are for your actions.

advise

A coach can **advise** you on how to improve your swimming.

What is a synonym for *advise*?

A synonym for advice is to help

desperately

The man tried **desperately** to remember where he parked the car.

Describe a time when you tried desperately to remember something.

_____

_____

hesitated

The cat **hesitated** before jumping off the table.

When have you hesitated before doing something?

_____

_____

humiliated

Isabel felt **humiliated** when she forgot her homework.

How is *humiliated* similar to *embarrassed*?

_____

_____

Build Your Word List Reread the third paragraph on page 41. **Circle** the word *curt*. Use a print or online dictionary to find the word's meaning, syllabication, and pronunciation. Write the meaning in your reader's notebook.

inspiration

The artist found **inspiration** in nature for her painting.

When you have to write a story, what gives you inspiration?

_____

_____

self-esteem

Scoring a goal in the game helped improve Billy's confidence and **self-esteem**.

What else builds self-esteem?

_____

_____

uncomfortably

Sonya's throat felt **uncomfortably** sore.

What are some things that can feel uncomfortably tight?

_____

_____

Idioms

Idioms are phrases that have a meaning different from the meaning of each word in the phrase. Sometimes context clues can help you figure out the meaning of an idiom.

FIND TEXT EVIDENCE

When I read the idiom see eye to eye *on page 39 in "The Talent Show," the words* After all, we are best friends *help me figure out its meaning. To* see eye to eye *means "to agree."*

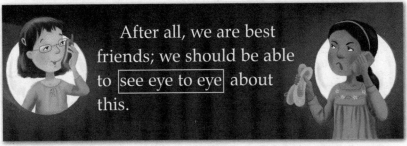

After all, we are best friends; we should be able to see eye to eye about this.

Your Turn Use context clues to help you figure out the meanings of the following idioms. Use an online resource to check your work.

cat got your tongue, page 40 _____

_____

standing up for myself, page 41 _____

_____

CHECK IN ⟩ 1 ⟩ 2 ⟩ 3 ⟩ 4 ⟩

Make Predictions

Use details in the story to predict what happens next or what you'll learn about a character. Read on to confirm, or check, your prediction. Correct your prediction if it is not right.

 FIND TEXT EVIDENCE

You probably predicted Tina is the kind of friend who is bossy. Reread page 39 of the story to find the text evidence that confirms your prediction.

Page 39

> During math, I tried to think of how I would tell Tina that I wanted to do my own act. After all, we are best friends; we should be able to see eye to eye about this. The problem is Tina always takes charge, I don't speak up, and then I end up feeling resentful about the whole situation.

I read that Tina always takes charge. This confirms my prediction that Tina is bossy.

 Your Turn Using clues you find in the text, how do you predict Maura will solve a future problem with her friends? As you read, use the strategy Make Predictions.

_____

_____

_____

CHECK IN 1 2 3 4

Plot

"The Talent Show" is realistic fiction. Realistic fiction is a made-up story that has settings, characters, and dialogue, or the exact words characters say, that could be real. It has a plot, or story events, that could really happen. A conflict, or problem, is introduced at the beginning of the story. The story ends when the conflict is resolved. Setting, events, conflict, and character development all contribute to, or affect, the plot.

🔍 **FIND TEXT EVIDENCE**

I can tell that "The Talent Show" is realistic fiction. Details about the school show it could be a real place. The characters say and do things real people might say and do. All the events could really happen.

Page 39

"Tina, there's a school talent show in three weeks," I shouted to my best friend. My older brother had been teaching me juggling, and I knew he'd help me with my act for the show.

Tina ran over to the bulletin board and read the poster. "Maura, what's our act going to be?" Tina asked me.

"Our act?" I said, taking a tighter grip on my books.

Tina grinned, pointed to the poster and said, "It says acts can be individuals, partners, or small groups."

My grip on my books became **uncomfortably** tight. "You want to do an act together?"

"It'll be fun," Tina said.

I **hesitated** for a second before continuing. "I've got an idea and . . ."

Tina interrupted me. "Yeah, me too; let's talk at lunch."

During math, I tried to think of how I would tell Tina that I wanted to do my own act. After all, we are best friends; we should be able to see eye to eye about this. The problem is Tina always takes charge, I don't speak up, and then I end up feeling resentful about the whole situation.

I **desperately** wanted to win, but it was more than that. I wanted to win on my own—with an act that was all mine.

Quick Tip

In a story, one event often leads to, or causes, another event. This series of events contributes to the plot.

Event Maura tells Tina that there will be a school talent show.

How it contributes to the plot: Tina reads a poster about the show and decides that she and Maura should do an act together.

⌐ **Plot** Plot is the sequence of events that
∟ make up a story.

👥 **Your Turn** With a partner, discuss how events in the story lead to other events and contribute to the plot. Chose one of those events and write how it contributes to the plot._____

_____

_____

_____

_____

CHECK IN ⟩ 1 ⟩ 2 ⟩ 3 ⟩ 4 ⟩

Plot: Conflict

The main character in a story often has a conflict, or problem, that needs to be solved, or resolved. The events caused by the conflict and the steps the character takes to resolve the conflict contribute to the story's plot.

🔍 FIND TEXT EVIDENCE

As I reread pages 39 and 40 of "The Talent Show," I can see that Maura has a problem. I will list the events in the story. Then I can figure out how Maura finds a solution, or resolution.

Character
Maura

Conflict
Maura does not want to do an act with her best friend Tina but is afraid to tell her.

Event
Maura tells Tina about her idea to do a juggling act. Tina dismisses the idea.

Event

Resolution

 Your Turn Reread "The Talent Show." Find other story events. Discuss how they contribute to the plot. Use these events to identify how the conflict is resolved. List them in the graphic organizer on page 47.

CHECK IN ▶ 1 〉 2 〉 3 〉 4 〉

Character

Maura

Conflict

Maura does not want to do an act with Tina but is afraid to tell her.

Event

Maura tells Tina about her idea to do a juggling act. Tina dismisses the idea.

Event

Resolution

My Goal
I can use text evidence to respond to realistic fiction.

Respond to Reading

COLLABORATE

Discuss the prompt below. Use your notes and text evidence to support your response.

What can readers learn from Maura?

CHECK IN 1 2 3 4

Solving a Community Problem

COLLABORATE

Positive things can happen when people take action to solve a problem. Write a formal letter to a state or local government official to describe a community problem and suggest a solution. Follow the research process. Work with a partner.

Step 1 **Set a Goal** Brainstorm problems in your community that you would like to see fixed. Choose one problem and write it down.

The problem is: _____

_____

Step 2 **Identify Sources** Use books, websites, newspapers, and other reliable sources to find information about the problem and how it was fixed in another community.

Step 3 **Find and Record Information** Gather your information. Take notes in your own words and cite your sources.

Step 4 **Organize and Synthesize Information** Plan your letter. First, state and explain the problem. Then tell about a possible solution. You might suggest that a group of community members be organized to work on it.

Step 5 **Create and Present** Write your letter. Include a proper greeting, body, complimentary close, and signature. Decide how you will present your letter to your class.

Wilton Q. Furmani
1234 Canyon Drive
Central City, AZ 00000

May 1, 2018

Ms. Viola Smart, President
Acme Corporation
100 Roadrunner Way
Central City, AZ 00000

Dear Ms. Smart:

I am a customer. I recently received your catalog and saw that you stopped selling trampolines. I need a new one and wanted to order it from your company. Will you be selling trampolines again in the future? If not, I wonder if you can tell me how to reach the manufacturer.

Thank you so much for your assistance on this matter.

Sincerely,

Wilton Q. Furmani
Wilton Q. Furmani

The example above shows a formal letter to a business. The same format and tone are used for most formal letters. **Circle** the greeting. Who is the writer of the letter? Write your answer below.

_____

_____

_____

CHECK IN ⟩ 1 ⟩ 2 ⟩ 3 ⟩ 4

Experts, Incorporated

? How does the author use dialogue to make the characters seem like people you might know in real life?

Literature Anthology: pages 24–33

COLLABORATE

Talk About It Reread the dialogue on page 25 of the **Literature Anthology**. Does the author do a good job using realistic dialogue between Rodney and his friends? Turn to your partner and talk about whether you agree or not.

Cite Text Evidence Find examples of realistic dialogue and write them in the chart. Write text evidence and explain if the dialogue is effective at making the characters seem like people you might know in real life.

Evaluate Information

Think about the way you speak. Compare it to the dialogue in the text. Which words sound similar to the words you use? Is the author's use of dialogue realistic?

Dialogue	Is It Effective?

Write The characters sound like people I might know because the author _____

_____

_____

CHECK IN 1 2 3 4

How does the author build tension when Rodney tries to think of what to write about?

 Talk About It Reread the third paragraph on page 29 in the **Literature Anthology**. Turn to a partner and talk about how the author describes what Rodney is thinking.

Cite Text Evidence How does the author help you understand how Rodney feels as he tries to think of an idea? Write clues in the web.

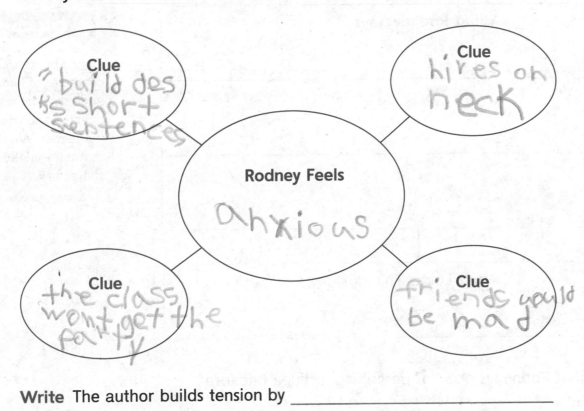

Clue
build des ts short sentences

Clue
hires on neck

Rodney Feels
anxious

Clue
the class wont get the party

Clue
friends would be mad

Write The author builds tension by _____

_____

_____

Quick Tip

I can use these sentence starters when we talk about how the author builds tension.

- *Some words the author uses to build tension in the story are . . .*
- *I can also look at . . .*

 Make Inferences

An inference is a decision you make about what you read based on the text evidence.

Think about the way Rodney acts when his friends ask him about his report. What inference can you make about the type of person he is? Do you think he feels bad about not having written the report? What makes you think that?

CHECK IN 1 2 3 4

How do you know that Rodney is good at defending and describing his idea to others?

 Talk About It Reread page 32 of the **Literature Anthology**. Talk with a partner about how Lucas reacts to Rodney's idea.

Cite Text Evidence How does Rodney convince Lucas that his idea is a good one? Write text evidence in the chart below.

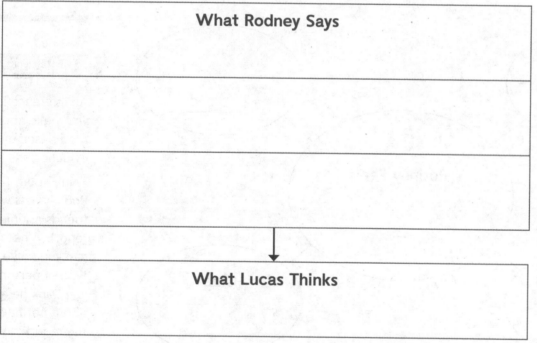

What Rodney Says

↓

What Lucas Thinks

Write I know that Rodney is good at describing his idea because _____

_____

_____

CHECK IN 1 2 3 4

Respond to Reading

COLLABORATE

Discuss the prompt below. Use your notes and text evidence to support your response.

What can readers learn from Rodney?

_____

_____

_____

_____

_____

_____

_____

_____

_____

_____

_____

_____

Quick Tip

Use these sentence starters to discuss the text and organize ideas.

- *One thing you can learn from Rodney is . . .*
- *For example, Rodney . . .*
- *This shows that . . .*

CHECK IN 1 2 3 4

Speaking Out to Stop Bullying

Literature Anthology:
pages 36–39

Communities Take a Stand

1   New Hampshire passed a law to stop bullies. The law states that <u>all school staff must be trained to know what bullying looks like</u>. People learn to spot the signs of bullying. <u>The law tells people who see bullying to report it</u>. <u>The state hopes that the law will create bully-free schools</u>.

2   In Midland, Texas, the police take their message to the schools. Police officers make sure to <u>tell students that bullying can be a crime</u>. They want bullies to know that they <u>are accountable for what they do</u>. This means that bullies will be punished if they <u>are caught</u>. The officers tell students who have been bullied or who have seen bullying <u>to report it right away</u>. They make it clear that people have choices. <u>They tell students that anyone can choose to stop being a bully</u>.

Reread paragraph 1. **Circle** the sentences that describe the law New Hampshire has about bullying. Write the sentences below.

The law trains people to know what bullying if the state hopes the law will create bully free schools.

COLLABORATE

Reread paragraph 2. Talk with a partner about the message police officers take to schools. **Underline** the three sentences that police officers tell students about bullying.

Young People Speak Out

[3] . . . Actress Lauren Potter has a message for lawmakers. She has been speaking out about the bullying of special-needs students. Lauren was born with Down syndrome. Because she did not look like her classmates, she was teased and called names as a child. She wants laws that will keep people safe from bullies.

Learning to Speak Up

[4] It is important for people everywhere to recognize and stand up to all forms of bullying. Everyone has a right to feel safe and to be treated with respect. Likewise, each person has a responsibility to treat others with respect. Report anything that may get in the way of maintaining a safe environment.

Reread paragraph 3. **Underline** the sentence that tells what Lauren Potter speaks out about to lawmakers.

COLLABORATE

Reread paragraph 4. Talk with a partner about what the author is saying you can do to stop bullying. **Draw a box** around the sentence that supports your response. Write the sentence below.

_____

_____

_____

How do you know how the author feels about bullying?

Talk About It Look back at the excerpts on pages 54 and 55. Talk about how the author feels about bullying.

Cite Text Evidence What clues help you understand the author's feelings about bullying? Write text evidence here.

Text Evidence	→	How the Author Feels
	→	
	→	

Write The author helps me understand how he or she feels about bullying by _____

_____

_____

_____

CHECK IN 〉1〉2〉3〉4〉

Author's Claim

When authors want to convince readers of an idea, they often make a claim, or state their belief about the idea. A claim is a statement that something is true, though others may not agree. Authors support their claims with reasons and evidence. Evidence includes facts and details.

FIND TEXT EVIDENCE

On page 37 of "Speaking Out to Stop Bullying" in the **Literature Anthology**, the author makes a claim in the first sentence. "One of the toughest issues facing students today is bullying." After defining the meaning of bullying, the author gives a reason that supports the claim. The reason is "The victim usually feels powerless." The rest of the paragraph gives evidence that supports this reason.

A bully's power may stem from being older, bigger, or stronger. **Bullies may also seem to have more resources than the person they target.**

Your Turn Reread page 55.

- What claim does the author make?

_____

_____

- What is a reason the author gives to support the claim?

_____

Readers to Writers

When you write a claim, make sure it is clearly stated. Check that your reasons and evidence are all related to your claim and support your perspective, or position. Remember, your goal is to convince your readers of an idea or belief.

COLLABORATE

? How do the girls in the photograph below and the selections *Experts, Incorporated* and "Speaking Out to Stop Bullying" help you understand how your actions might affect others?

Talk About It Read the caption and look at the photograph. Talk with a partner about what the girls are doing.

Cite Text Evidence What clues help you see how the older girl is affecting the life of the younger girl? **Circle** them in the photograph. Reread the caption and **underline** text evidence that tells why the two girls are together.

Write The photograph and the selections help me understand how my actions could affect others by _____

_____

_____

_____

_____

_____

Quick Tip

When you read, use clues in photographs and illustrations to help you better understand the text. For example, look at the actions of the people. The expressions on their faces can tell you how they feel.

The two girls are both part of a program in their community that teams older students with younger ones. The younger girl is learning to play baseball.

Eric McNatt/Stockbyte/Getty Images

CHECK IN 1 2 3 4

Write an Essay

Think about what you learned about how our actions can affect others. Why is it important to be aware of how our actions affect others?

1 Look at your Build Knowledge notes in your reader's notebook.

2 Write your ideas about why it is important to be aware of how our actions affect others. What helps us better understand the possible effects of our actions? Include text evidence that supports your ideas.

3 Use your ideas to write an essay explaining why it is important to be aware of how our actions affect others. Use new vocabulary words in your essay.

Think about what you learned in this text set. Fill in the bars on page 37.

Build Knowledge

Build Vocabulary

Write new words you learned about how starting a business can help others. Draw lines and circles for the words you write.

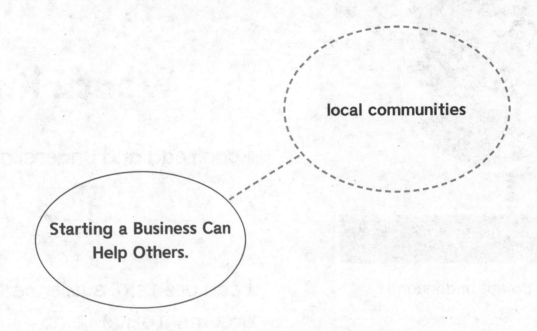

local communities

Starting a Business Can Help Others.

Go online to **my.mheducation.com** and read the "Helping Others Is Good Business" Blast. Think about how these businesses help people and make money. Then blast back your response.

Think about what you already know. Fill in the bars. You'll keep learning more.

What I Know Now

Key
1 = I do not understand.
2 = I understand but need more practice.
3 = I understand.
4 = I understand and can teach someone.

I can read and understand argumentative text.

1 > 2 > 3 > 4

I can use text evidence to respond to argumentative text.

1 > 2 > 3 > 4

I know how starting a business can help others.

1 > 2 > 3 > 4

STOP You will come back to the next page later.

What I Learned

I can read and understand argumentative text.

| 1 | 2 | 3 | 4 |

I can use text evidence to respond to argumentative text.

| 1 | 2 | 3 | 4 |

I know how starting a business can help others.

| 1 | 2 | 3 | 4 |

SHARED READ

My Goal I can read and understand argumentative text.

TAKE NOTES

As you read, make note of interesting words and important information.

_____

_____

_____

_____

_____

_____

_____

_____

_____

_____

_____

_____

_____

Essential Question

?

How can starting a business help others?

Read about how two companies are making a difference.

Kwaku Alston/Stockland Martel

Dollars and $ENSE

centralidea

Behind the success of these big businesses is a desire to help others.

Good business is not always about the bottom line. A **compassionate** company knows that making money is not the only way to measure success. Many large businesses in the United States and all over the world are finding unusual ways to help people in need.

Hearts and Soles

After starting and running four businesses, Blake Mycoskie wanted a break from his usual **routine**. In 2006, he traveled to Argentina, in South America, and while he was there he learned to sail and to dance. He also visited poor villages where very few of the children had shoes. Mycoskie decided he had to do something. "I'm going to start a shoe company, and for every pair I sell, I'm going to give one pair to a kid in need."

For this inventive new **undertaking**, Mycoskie started the business using his own money. He named it TOMS: Shoes for Tomorrow. The slip-on shoes are modeled on shoes that are traditionally worn by Argentine workers.

Mycoskie immediately set up his **innovative** one-for-one program. TOMS gives away one pair of shoes for every pair that is purchased. Later that year, Mycoskie returned to Argentina and gave away 10,000 pairs of shoes. By 2016, TOMS had donated over 60 million pairs.

Unit 1 • Text Set 3   65

ARGUMENTATIVE TEXT

FIND TEXT EVIDENCE

Read

Paragraph 1

Central Idea and Details

Underline the central, or main, idea of the first paragraph.

Paragraphs 2–4

Reread

Circle the details that tell you what Mycoskie noticed when he visited villages in Argentina. What did this cause him to do?

Suffixes

The suffix *-ive* means "related or belonging to." **Draw a box** around the word in the third paragraph with the suffix *-ive*.

Reread

Author's Craft

What is the author's purpose for using "Sense" instead of "Cents" in the title "Dollars and Sense"?

TOMS' employees unpack shoes to give away.

FIND TEXT EVIDENCE

Read

Paragraphs 1–2

Reread

Circle the text evidence that shows what Mycoskie's company did next. What has this taught Mycoskie?

_____

_____

_____

Paragraphs 3–5

Central Idea and Details

Underline the detail that best explains one way Hard Rock Cafe raises money to give back to the community.

Reread

Author's Craft

How does the author's use of Blake Mycoskie's own words help support the author's claim that businesses can give back?

The company has expanded to sell eyeglasses. In a similar program, one pair of eyeglasses is donated for every pair that is bought.

Mycoskie is pleased and surprised. "I always thought I would spend the first half of my life making money and the second half giving it away," Mycoskie says. "I never thought I could do both at the same time."

Giving Back Rocks!

Have you ever seen a Hard Rock Cafe? The company runs restaurants and hotels. In 1990, the company launched a new **enterprise**: charity. Since then, it has given away millions of dollars to different causes. Its motto is Love All, Serve All.

One way the company raises **funds** for charity is by selling a line of T-shirts. The **process** starts with rock stars designing the art that goes on the shirts. Then the shirts are sold on the Internet. Part of the money that is raised from the sales of the shirts is given to charity.

Employees at Hard Rock Cafe locations are encouraged to raise money for their community. Every store does it differently.

Hard Rock Cafes are committed to giving back to the community.

Top Five Charities

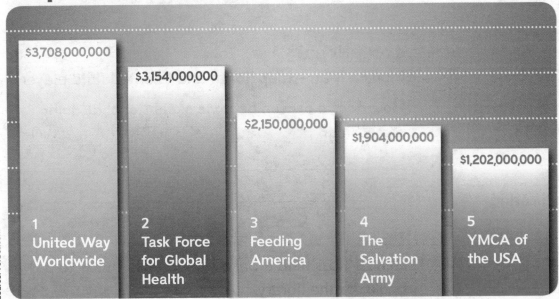

Source: Forbes.com

$3,708,000,000	$3,154,000,000	$2,150,000,000	$1,904,000,000	$1,202,000,000
1 United Way Worldwide	2 Task Force for Global Health	3 Feeding America	4 The Salvation Army	5 YMCA of the USA

Individuals as well as businesses are committed to helping people in need. This graph shows the American charities that got the most donations in 2016 and how much money they raised.

The restaurant in Hollywood, Florida, worked with some **exceptional** students from two Florida high schools. Together, they put on an event to raise money for the Make-A-Wish Foundation. The foundation grants wishes to children with serious medical problems.

The Bottom Line

Every day companies are thinking of innovative ways to give back to their community.

If you own a business, making a profit is a necessity. However, helping others is just as important as the bottom line. Helping others is good business!

> ## Summarize
>
> Use your notes, the headings, the graph, and the photographs to summarize the information in "Dollars and Sense."

FIND TEXT EVIDENCE

Read

Graphs and Headings

Underline the heading on the graph. Which charity donated the most in 2016? Write it below.

_____

_____

Paragraphs 1–2

Central Idea and Details

Draw a box around the sentence that summarizes the central idea.

Reread

Author's Craft

The "bottom line" refers to profit a business makes. It also means the central, or main, idea of something. How does the play on words in the heading relate to the text?

Vocabulary

Use the example sentences to talk with a partner about each word. Then answer the questions.

compassionate

I could tell Milo was a **compassionate** and caring person by the way he hugged his brother.

What is an antonym for *compassionate*?

_____

_____

enterprise

Starting a white-water rafting business was an exciting new **enterprise** for Reynaldo.

What new enterprises are there in your community?

_____

_____

exceptional

Monica is an **exceptional** and talented flute player.

How does a person become exceptional at doing something?

_____

_____

funds

Elena's class held a bake sale to raise **funds** to buy books for the library.

What project would you like to raise funds for?

_____

_____

innovative

Ming enjoyed trying out the **innovative** new wheelchair.

What new technology do you think was innovative for its time?

_____

_____

 Build Your Word List Underline a word in "Dollars and Sense" that you find interesting. In your reader's notebook, make a word web of different forms of the word. Use a print or online dictionary to look up the meanings of each word. Many online dictionaries let you listen to words' pronunciation and syllabication as well.

process

An important step in the **process** of making a pie is to roll out the crust.

What is one step in the process of baking cookies?

_____

_____

routine

Barak loved the daily **routine** of walking his dog.

Why is it helpful to have a morning routine?

_____

_____

undertaking

Cleaning up Tim's messy bedroom was going to be a big **undertaking**.

What would you consider a big undertaking?

_____

_____

Suffixes

A suffix is a word part added to the end of a word to change its meaning and often its part of speech. Look at the suffixes below.

-*ly* = "done in the way of"
-*ive* = "related or belonging to"
-*ity* = "state or quality of"

🔍 FIND TEXT EVIDENCE

I see the word innovative *on page 65 of "Dollars and Sense." Looking at its word parts, I see the base word* innovate. *The suffix* -ive *changes the verb* innovate *into an adjective. This suffix will help me figure out what* innovative *means.*

Mycoskie immediately set up his innovative one-for-one program.

Your Turn Use suffixes and context clues to figure out the meanings of the following words:

traditionally, page 65 _____

immediately, page 65 _____

necessity, page 67 _____

CHECK IN ⟩ 1 ⟩ 2 ⟩ 3 ⟩ 4 ⟩

Reread

When you read an argumentative text, you may come across ideas and information that are new to you. As you read "Dollars and Sense," reread sections to make sure you understand the important facts and details in the text.

 FIND TEXT EVIDENCE

As you read, you may want to make sure you understand the ways a business can help others. Reread the section "Hearts and Soles" in "Dollars and Sense."

Page 65

Mycoskie decided he had to do something. "I'm going to start a shoe company, and for every pair I sell, I'm going to give one pair to a kid in need."

I read that TOMS gives away one pair of shoes for every pair of shoes that someone buys. From this text evidence, I can draw the inference that the more shoes TOMS sells, the more shoes can be given away.

 Your Turn What is another example of a company giving back to the community? Reread page 66 to answer the question. As you read other selections, remember to use the strategy Reread.

_____

_____

_____

Ariel Skelley/Blend Images

CHECK IN 1 2 3 4

Graphs and Headings

"Dollars and Sense" is an example of argumentative text. It includes reasons and evidence that support a claim, or argument. Argumentative texts may include text features, such as **graphs** and **headings**.

FIND TEXT EVIDENCE

"Dollars and Sense" states the author's claim and tries to get readers to agree. It includes headings, as well as a graph that shows the amount of money raised by different charities.

Page 67

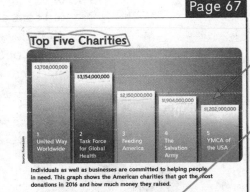

Graphs help you picture numerical information. This bar graph helps you compare information.

Headings tell you what the section is mostly about.

Your Turn Find and list ⟨two⟩ text features in "Dollars and Sense." Tell what information you learned from each of the features.

photos, captions, bar graph

Central Idea and Relevant Details

The central idea is the author's most important thoughts, or main point, about a topic or subject. A relevant detail gives information that tells more about the topic and supports the central idea.

FIND TEXT EVIDENCE

To identify the central idea of "Giving Back Rocks!" on page 66, I'll think about the topic of the article, how businesses can help others. Then, I'll look for details that are relevant, or related to the topic. Next I will evaluate what the details have in common to identify the central idea.

Central Idea
Hard Rock Cafe is a company that gives money to charity.
Detail
Hard Rock Cafe sells a line of T-shirts to raise funds for charity.
Detail
The shirts are sold on the Internet.
Detail
Part of the money that is raised from the sales of the shirts is given to charity.

Your Turn Reread the section "Hearts and Soles" on pages 65–66. Find the relevant details in the section and list them in your graphic organizer on page 73. Use the details to identify the central idea. Explain to your partner how the details support the central idea.

Quick Tip

A central idea may or may not be directly stated in a text.

When the central idea is not directly stated, ask yourself, "What does the author most want readers to know or understand?" You can often use headings as clues. Then check to see if the details support your ideas.

To better understand a stated central idea, look for the relevant details and think about how they support that central idea.

CHECK IN ⟩ 1 ⟩ 2 ⟩ 3 ⟩ 4

Central Idea Blake wanted to help children without shoes.
Detail He started a company called Toms.
Detail For every pair purechased one is donated.
Detail Toms donated 60 million pairs.

Respond to Reading

COLLABORATE

Discuss the prompt below. Use your notes and text evidence to support your response.

Do you agree with the author's claim that businesses can help others? Explain your answer.

_____

_____

_____

_____

_____

_____

_____

_____

_____

_____

_____

_____

_____

_____

_____

Quick Tip

Use these sentence starters to discuss the text and organize your ideas.

- _I think that businesses . . ._
- _Examples of this are . . ._
- _This shows that . . ._

Grammar Connection

Check your use of compound subjects. A compound subject is two or more subjects with the same predicate.

The subjects are usually joined by **and** or **or**: _Sally and Henry ate apples._

If there are three or more subjects, they are separated by commas: _Sally, Henry, and Ann ate apples._

CHECK IN 1 2 3 4

Businesses That Help Others

Follow the research process to write a biographical report about a business leader or entrepreneur who created a business that helped others. Work with a partner.

Step 1 **Set a Goal** As part of your research, you'll find and choose a person to write about. List questions you want your research to answer.

Step 2 **Identify Sources** Scan books or websites to find examples of entrepreneurs or business leaders. Choose one person who interests you. Then, use both primary and secondary sources to find information about the person and his or her business.

Step 3 **Find and Record Information** Take notes in your own words. Look for images you might want to include. Remember to include information not only about your chosen business leader but also about how the business has helped others. Cite where your information came from and create a list of sources.

Step 4 **Organize and Synthesize Information** Organize your notes. Make sure you introduce your subject at the beginning of your report.

Step 5 **Create and Present** Write your biographical report and decide how you will present it to the class.

Quick Tip

A primary source may be an original document or an account by someone who took part in an event.

Secondary sources are created by someone who doesn't have firsthand knowledge of the topic. Secondary sources include textbooks and encyclopedias.

The image above shows two primary sources: an old photograph and a diary. What else could be a primary source?

_____

_____

CHECK IN 1 2 3 4

Kids in Business

 How does the author help you understand how he or she feels about young entrepreneurs?

Literature Anthology: pages 40–43

 Talk About It Reread **Literature Anthology** page 41. Turn to a partner and talk about Hayleigh's and Joshua's businesses.

Cite Text Evidence What phrases show how the author feels about what Hayleigh and Joshua are doing? Write text evidence in the chart.

Text Evidence	How the Author Feels

The intended audience for "Kids in Business" is _____

Write The author shows how he or she feels about young

entrepreneurs by _____

_____

_____

 Make Inferences

Authors use specific words that give clues about how they feel about a topic. As you read, think about whether the author's words are positive or negative. A word such as *enterprise* has a positive connotation, or feeling. The word *dull* has a negative connotation, or feeling. To make an inference, use evidence from the text and your own knowledge of the topic to come to a new understanding of the text.

CHECK IN 〉1〉2〉3〉4〉

? **Why does the author use a graph to help you see how effective Better World Books has been at raising money?**

Talk About It Reread **Literature Anthology** page 43. With your partner, talk about what you learned by looking at the graph.

Cite Text Evidence How does the graph help you understand how donating books can make a difference? Write text evidence.

How Better World Books Works	What the Graph Shows	What the Graph Means

Write The author uses a graph to help me _____

_____

_____

Evaluate Information

When you read a text, take time to evaluate the details the author provides. This will help you to determine the relevant ideas in the text.

Look at the graph. What do you notice about the sales of books over the years? What do you predict a graph of years after 2014 will show?

CHECK IN 〉 1 〉 2 〉 3 〉 4 〉

Respond to Reading

Discuss the prompt below. Use your notes and text evidence to support your response.

How can kids take initiative and start businesses that are helpful?

_____

_____

_____

_____

_____

_____

_____

_____

_____

_____

_____

_____

Quick Tip

Use these sentence starters to talk about and cite evidence in the text.

- *One way kids can take initiative is . . .*
- *This business helps others because . . .*
- *Other ways to take initiative and start a helpful business are . . .*

CHECK IN 1 2 3 4

*Literature Anthology:
pages 44–45*

Starting a Successful Business

[1] Becoming an entrepreneur is hard work. But if you're dedicated and have excellent organizational skills, it can be rewarding—sometimes, a small idea can become a very successful business! Neale S. Godfrey, author of *Ultimate Kids' Money Book*, shares these tips for a booming business.

[2] **Step 1 Have an innovative idea.**

Suppose you like dogs, have free time, and feel compassionate toward people with busy schedules. Why not start a dog-walking service?

Reread and use the prompts to take notes in the text.

Underline words and phrases in paragraph 1 that tell what the author thinks about what it takes to become an entrepreneur. Write them here.

1 _____

2 _____

3 _____

COLLABORATE

Reread paragraph 2. Talk with a partner about how the author helps you understand what the word *innovative* means.

Circle clues in the illustration that support the text.

How do the illustrations help you understand the steps to starting a business?

 Talk About It Reread the excerpt on page 79. Talk with a partner about the illustration and what it shows.

Cite Text Evidence What extra information do you get from the picture? Write clues in the chart.

Text Evidence	Picture Clues

Write The illustration helps me learn more about

starting a business by _____

_____

_____

_____

_____

Evaluate Information

Evaluating the photographs and illustrations in a text helps you better understand what you are reading. Ask yourself these questions.

- *Why did the author include this image?*
- *What does the image help me understand about the topic?*

CHECK IN ▷ 1 ▷ 2 ▷ 3 ▷ 4

Sequence

Authors can use a **sequence** text structure to explain how to do something in order or as steps in a process. A sequence text structure often includes

- instructions on how to do something
- labeled or numbered steps
- pictures or diagrams showing materials or how to perform a step

FIND TEXT EVIDENCE

On page 45 in "Starting a Successful Business" in the **Literature Anthology,** the author uses a sequence text structure to explain how to be a young entrepreneur. By numbering and describing each step of the process, the author explains the steps in a clear way.

> Step 1 Have an innovative idea.
>
> Step 2 Find out if your business has a chance of succeeding.
>
> Step 3 Compile a business plan and a budget.
>
> Step 4 Contact potential customers.
>
> Step 5 Keep tabs on your business.

Your Turn Reread the steps you can take to start a business on page 45 of the Literature Anthology.

- How does the sequence text structure affect what you think about

  starting a business? _____

  _____

Readers to Writers

You can use a sequence text structure in your own writing. If you want to explain a process or how to do something, consider numbering the different steps in the process. You can also make a chart of the different steps and add pictures to illustrate each step.

? **How is the information in the photograph similar to the information in "Kids in Business" and "Starting a Successful Business"?**

Talk About It Look at the photo. Read the caption. With a partner, talk about what the people are doing and why they are doing it. How is what they are doing similar to starting a business?

Cite Text Evidence Circle clues in the caption and photograph that let you know what is happening and why.

Write The photograph and the selections all give information about _____

_____

_____

_____

_____

_____

_____

_____

_____

_____

Quick Tip

Compare the information in the photo to the information in the selections. What does the information have in common with both selections? What does it have in common with only one of the selections?

The girl and teacher in this photo are helping to set up a bake sale to raise money for their school.

CHECK IN 1 2 3 4

My Goal **I know how starting a business can help others.**

Write an Editorial

Think about what you learned about how starting a business can help others. How can this information be used to inspire businesses to help others? Write an argumentative piece for a newspaper telling why businesses should help others.

1 Look at your Build Knowledge notes in your reader's notebook.

2 Choose at least three businesses that you read about to use as examples of why businesses should help others.

3 Write your argumentative piece. Include new vocabulary words. Cite text evidence to support your ideas. Remember, your goal is to convince businesses to help others.

Think about what you learned in this text set. Fill in the bars on page 63.

Think about what you already know. Then fill in the bars. Meeting your goals may take time.

Key	
1 =	I do not understand.
2 =	I understand but need more practice.
3 =	I understand.
4 =	I understand and can teach someone.

What I Know Now

I can write an argumentative essay.

> 1 > 2 > 3 > 4 >

I can synthesize information from three sources.

> 1 > 2 > 3 > 4 >

Think about what you've learned. Fill in the bars. What do you want to work on more?

What I Learned

I can write an argumentative essay.

1 > 2 > 3 > 4

I can synthesize information from three sources.

1 > 2 > 3 > 4

WRITE TO SOURCES

You will answer an argumentative writing prompt using sources and a rubric.

ANALYZE THE RUBRIC

A rubric tells you what needs to be included in your writing.

Purpose, Focus, and Organization
Read the second bullet. What should a claim clearly support?

_____

_____

_____

Evidence and Elaboration
Read the second bullet. Where can you get examples of relevant evidence?

_____

_____

_____

Evidence and Elaboration
Underline the words in the third bullet that tell you what some elaborative techniques are.

Argumentative Writing Rubric

Purpose, Focus, and Organization • Score 4

- stays focused on the purpose, audience, and task
- **makes a claim that clearly supports a perspective**
- uses transitional strategies, such as words and phrases, to connect ideas
- presents ideas in a logical progression, or order
- begins with a strong introduction and ends with a strong conclusion

Evidence and Elaboration • Score 4

- effectively supports the claim with logical reasons
- has strong examples of relevant evidence, or supporting details, from multiple sources
- uses elaborative techniques, such as examples, definitions, and quotations from sources
- expresses interesting ideas clearly using precise language
- uses appropriate academic and domain-specific language
- uses different sentence structures

Turn to page 236 for the complete Argumentative Writing Rubric.

Shutterstock/Valentain Jevee

Make a Claim

Purpose

The purpose of an argumentative essay is to persuade or convince the reader to think a certain way about a topic. In order to do this, the writer presents an argument that includes a clearly stated claim, logical reasons, and relevant evidence, such as facts and examples.

Make a Claim A strong claim clearly states an opinion or belief about a topic. The claim should support the writer's perspective, or position, on the topic. The claim also lets readers know what the essay will be about.

> **If there is a natural disaster, such as a wildfire or hurricane, everyone should evacuate.** People who refuse to leave their homes during an emergency put their own lives at risk. They also put at risk the lives of rescue workers who may be asked to save them during the emergency.

Read the above paragraph. The claim is highlighted. What does the claim tell you about the topic of the essay?

If there is a natural disaster everyone should evacuate.

Perspective Writers use reasons and evidence to support their claims. These reasons and evidence tell more about the writer's perspective on the topic. Circle the reasons the writer gives for the claim. What do these reasons help you understand about the writer's perspective?

These reasons help me understand why the writer to evacuate.

ANALYZE THE STUDENT MODEL

Paragraph 1

Write a detail from Maria's introduction that caught your attention.

category 5 hurricane has winds over 157 mph...

Read the first paragraph of Maria's essay. The claim is highlighted.

Paragraph 2

What is an example of relevant evidence that Maria uses to support her claim?

_____

_____

_____

Circle the problems people may have after a storm.

Student Model: Argumentative Essay

Maria responded to the Writing Prompt: *Write an argumentative essay for your local newspaper about whether people should be forced to evacuate during a hurricane.* Read Maria's essay below.

1   The United States has many hurricanes. In fact, hurricanes have hit all states on the Gulf and Atlantic Coasts. According to the Saffir-Simpson scale, hurricanes are rated from 1 to 5. A Category 5 hurricane has winds over 157 mph and strong storm surges. If a hurricane is a Category 4 or 5, a city or county may issue a mandatory evacuation order. This means that everyone must leave. However, some people refuse to go. It's impossible to make everyone evacuate. Even if you could force everyone to leave, the evacuation can cause problems.

2   After the storm is over, millions of people can be left with no power, no drinking water, and a flooded house. So why do people decide to stay? If people are elderly or disabled, they may have nobody to help them leave. Some people don't have the money for gas. Others think that their houses are safe because they have been through a hurricane before. Then there are people who won't leave their pets behind because most emergency shelters won't take pets. I can't imagine leaving my cat behind if I had to evacuate.

3   Getting millions of people out is not easy and can cause lots of problems. In the article "No Good Choice," the author tells about the city of Houston, Texas. The city tried to evacuate 2.5 million people during Hurricane Rita in 2005. There was a 100-mile traffic jam. Some people ran out of gas and had to leave their cars. When Hurricane Irma was heading straight toward Florida in 2017, the Department of Emergency Management ordered about 6.3 million people to evacuate. How can there possibly be enough police officers to force millions of people to leave? Millions of people did evacuate. The traffic jams were horrible, and as the storm approached, road conditions became dangerous.

4   I wish there was a way for everyone to evacuate during a hurricane, but I do not see how you can force people to leave. During Hurricane Harvey in 2017, a Category 4 storm, my grandmother decided to follow her county's mandatory evacuation. She went to stay with her cousin. I'm glad she did because her house was destroyed. People have many different reasons for staying in their homes. However, we all need to work on better evacuation plans for those people who do want to leave.

ARGUMENTATIVE ESSAY

Paragraph 3

Reread the third paragraph. **Underline** the question. How does this technique of elaboration support Maria's claim in paragraph 1?

_____

_____

_____

Paragraph 4

What is an example of domain-specific vocabulary that Maria uses in paragraph 4?

_____

_____

_____

Reread Maria's claim in paragraph 1. **Circle** the sentence in paragraph 4 that restates Maria's claim.

Apply the Rubric

With a partner, use the rubric on page 86 to discuss why Maria scored a 4 on her essay.

Analyze the Prompt

Writing Prompt

Write an argumentative essay to present to your class about whether people should build in flood zones.

Purpose, Audience, and Task Reread the writing prompt. What is your purpose for writing? My purpose is to ___persude___

Who will your audience be? My audience will be ___class___

What type of writing is the prompt asking for? ___argumentative___

Set a Purpose for Reading Sources Asking questions about the pros and cons of building in a flood zone will help you figure out your purpose for reading. Before you read the passage set about building in flood zones, write a question here.

___What problems are there for people who build in flood zones___

Read the following passage set.

HOW TO BUILD IN FLOOD ZONES

1   Every year, many people visit the coast of South Carolina. They come to enjoy our beaches and the natural beauty. People have built homes and businesses along the coasts for many years. **We can't stop people from building in flood zones.** Besides, building more houses and businesses means more jobs for everyone.

2   Yesterday, I read an article in your newspaper that said many people are worried about flood zones. The article said some coastal South Carolina areas have too much floodplain development. It also said that developers too often use fill dirt to make a building site higher. Studies show that fill dirt in the wrong places leads to problems. It can actually cause greater flooding in nearby areas. That flooding causes costly damage.

3   Hurricanes and floods are part of life in South Carolina. They can be destructive, but there is a solution. In flood zones, there should be rules and laws about when to use columns to raise a building. Homes can be built above the ground and be protected from floods, as the photograph below shows. They can also be constructed to withstand hurricanes with storm-resistant doors and windows. This will also help prevent extra flooding caused by fill dirt. It may be expensive to elevate a building. But the cost of rebuilding after a flood can be even more expensive. People will continue to build in flood zones, so let's make sure they will be as safe as possible.

poupine/Shutterstock

ARGUMENTATIVE ESSAY

FIND TEXT EVIDENCE

Paragraph 1

Reread paragraph 1. The claim is highlighted. What does the author think is a good thing about building in flood zones?

More jobs

Paragraph 2

Underline how some developers use fill dirt. What problems can using fill dirt cause?

It can cause greater greater flooding in near he arby areas.

Paragraph 3

Draw a box around what the author thinks is a solution to the problem of building in a flood zone. What does the author think is more expensive than raising a building?

Rebuilding after a flood.

Take Notes Paraphrase the author's claim and give examples of supporting details.

FIND TEXT EVIDENCE

Paragraph 4

Read the highlighted claim. What will the author try to convince the reader to think?

why people shouldn't build in flood zones

Paragraph 5

Circle the greatest threat during a hurricane. Why is it so dangerous?

storm surges can move entire buildings.

Paragraphs 6–8

Underline the detail that tells why natural floodplains are important. Why does FEMA want to create more wetlands?

_____

_____

Take Notes Paraphrase the author's argument, including examples of reasons and evidence.

SOURCE 2

More Wetlands Needed

4   North Carolina has a beautiful coastline. It is no wonder people want to live here. **But people shouldn't keep building more houses in flood zones.**

5   Hurricanes are a part of life in coastal North Carolina and have caused major damage. A storm surge is the greatest threat during a hurricane. This happens when ocean water rises very high. Powerful hurricane winds push the water onto land. A storm surge can move entire buildings.

6   North Carolina has natural floodplains that help to create a barrier from powerful storms. The marshlands surrounding Currituck Sound are an example of a natural floodplain. But for many years, developers have built houses and businesses in areas near the sound. It is important for developers to remember that natural wetlands are necessary to protect people from storms.

7   The Federal Emergency Management Agency (FEMA) is a government agency. It responds to disasters. FEMA wants to create more wetlands to help reduce flooding. Communities can reduce flooding by preserving and reconstructing nearby coastal marshes. The marshes will also help protect people farther inland.

8   Careful planning of flood zones is the best way to protect people and property from hurricanes. Creating wetlands will improve the environment and protect people from floods.

Debate on Flood Zones

9   Everyone knows that hurricanes and flooding can cause great damage to people and property. Should people continue building in Louisiana flood zones? Developers say "yes," and environmentalists say "no."

10   Developers say more homes and businesses are needed for the growing population. The businesses will create more jobs, too. This is good for Louisiana. They argue that developers already follow rules to make new buildings as safe as they can be. They make sure buildings in dangerous flood zones are raised several feet from the ground. Elevated buildings can help to protect against flooding.

11   However, environmentalists think preserving and reconstructing natural wetlands is a better way to protect people against floods. If people do not protect the wetlands, Louisiana's shore will eventually disappear. The Environmental Protection Agency says that the effectiveness of wetlands to reduce flooding varies. It depends on the size and location of the area. For example, a 1-acre wetland can store about 1 million gallons of water. The kind of soil and vegetation in the area is important, too. Wetlands provide a natural barrier that protects homes and businesses from storm damage. They are also homes for plants and animals.

12   There are no easy answers. Developers and environmentalists will need to decide together what southern Louisiana's flood zones will look like in the future.

Jocelyn Augustino/FEMA

ARGUMENTATIVE ESSAY

FIND TEXT EVIDENCE

Paragraph 9
Underline the two groups that the author will discuss in this essay.

Paragraph 10
Circle the reason that developers give for continuing to build in flood zones. What does the author think will help protect buildings against flooding?

_____

_____

_____

Paragraphs 11–12
Draw a box around how much water a 1-acre wetland can store. What is an important reason wetlands are needed in flood zones?

_____

_____

Take Notes Paraphrase the reasons that developers and environmentalists give for their claims about flood zones.

WRITING

TAKE NOTES

Read the writing prompt below. Write your claim. Then use the three sources, your notes, and the graphic organizer to plan a response.

Writing Prompt *Write an argumentative essay to present to your class about whether people should build in flood zones.*

Synthesize Information

Review the notes you took on each source. What role do wetlands play in flood zones? Discuss your ideas with your partner.

CHECK IN ⟩ 1 ⟩ 2 ⟩ 3 ⟩ 4 ⟩

Plan: Organize Ideas

Claim	Reasons
Building in a flood zone is (a good idea/~~a bad idea~~) because . . . Floods cause major damage that faka a lot of time and money to repair.	One reason that building in a flood zone is . . . bad is because it can be expensive to repair damages
	Another reason is it can be difficult to build a flood proof house
	There are not enough wetlands to protect hom from herrica

Relevant Evidence

Source 1	Source 2	Source 3
Flood damage can really expensive - millionto	Storn surges move entire building	
there should be a law that		Budings should be elevated
	FEMA wats more wetiands to help predt flooding	chage+action wet-pand Potet people form floods

Draft: Relevant Evidence

Choose Evidence Writers support their claims with logical reasons and relevant evidence, or supporting details, from multiple sources. Relevant evidence includes facts and examples that support your claim. In the paragraph below from Maria's argumentative essay on page 89, Maria presents relevant evidence from the source "No Good Choice." She picked this evidence to prove her argument that evacuations can cause problems.

> Getting millions of people out is not easy and can cause lots of problems. In the article "No Good Choice," the author tells about the city of Houston, Texas. The city tried to evacuate 2.5 million people during Hurricane Rita in 2005. There was a 100-mile traffic jam. Some people ran out of gas and had to leave their cars.

Draw a box around the claim in the paragraph. **Underline** the evidence that supports the claim. How does the paragraph provide evidence that supports Maria's argument that evacuations can cause problems? Write your answer below.

_____

_____

_____

Draft Use your graphic organizer to write your draft in your writer's notebook. Before you start writing, review the rubric on page 86. Remember to indent each paragraph and to put quotation marks around titles of articles.

Nata Studio/Shutterstock

Quick Tip

When using evidence from a source, you can directly quote a source or you can paraphrase the information.

Quotes When you quote from a source, you are using the exact words of the source. Put quotation marks around the quote.

Paraphrasing When you paraphrase, you are restating the information in your own words.

Citing Sources Remember to correctly cite the sources you've quoted, paraphrased, or used for information.

CHECK IN 1 2 3 4

Revise: Peer Conferences

Review a Draft Listen actively to your partner. Take notes about what you liked and what was difficult to follow. Begin by telling what you liked. Use these sentence starters.

Your claim was persuasive because . . .
What did you mean by . . .
I think adding more facts can help to . . .

After you give each other feedback, reflect on the peer conference. How can you use the guidance from your partner to help improve your writing?

Revision Use the Revising Checklist to help you figure out what text you may need to move, elaborate on, or delete. After you finish writing your final draft, use the full rubric on pages 236–239 to score your essay.

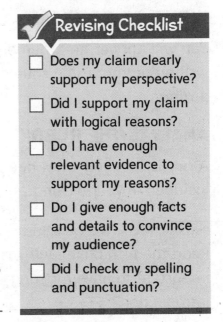

Next, you'll write an argumentative essay on a new topic.

My Score			
Purpose, Focus, & Organization (4 pts)	Evidence & Elaboration (4 pts)	Conventions (2 pts)	Total (10 pts)

WRITE TO SOURCES

You will answer an argumentative writing prompt using sources and a rubric.

ANALYZE THE RUBRIC

A rubric tells you what needs to be included in your writing.

Purpose, Focus, and Organization
Read the fifth bullet. Why is it important to have a strong introduction?

_____

_____

_____

Evidence and Elaboration
Read the third bullet. The base word of *elaborative* is *elaborate*. What is a synonym for the verb *to elaborate?*

_____

Evidence and Elaboration
Underline the words in the fourth bullet that tell you what to use to express ideas clearly.

Argumentative Writing Rubric

Purpose, Focus, and Organization • Score 4

- stays focused on the purpose, audience, and task
- makes a claim that clearly supports a perspective
- uses transitional strategies, such as words and phrases, to connect ideas
- presents ideas in a logical progression, or order
- begins with a strong introduction and ends with a strong conclusion

Evidence and Elaboration • Score 4

- effectively supports the claim with logical reasons
- has strong examples of relevant evidence, or supporting details, from multiple sources
- **uses elaborative techniques, such as examples, definitions, and quotations from sources**
- expresses interesting ideas clearly using precise language
- uses appropriate academic and domain-specific language
- uses different sentence structures

Turn to page 236 for the complete Argumentative Writing Rubric.

Valentain Jevee/Shutterstock

Elaboration

Explain and Build Writers use elaboration to build on and explain the evidence they present to support their claims. Some techniques of elaboration include quotations, definitions, descriptions, and examples. In the highlighted sentences below, the author uses an example to elaborate on the facts he presents.

According to "Facts About Colorado's Economy," in 2019 the travel industry directly supported about 180,000 jobs. **For example, my cousin works at a ski resort near Breckenridge. My uncle is a wilderness guide based in Boulder. Without the tourism industry, they would both be out of a job.**

Elaborate Now you try it. Read the sentence below. Use elaboration to help the reader understand more about apples. Pretend that your audience has never seen an apple before.

Apples are a fruit, and they grow on trees.

Apples can be yellow - red-green.

Writers have an audience in mind when they write. They make choices about what to include based on their audience. For example, if a scientist wrote an article for a kids' magazine, what might she include to help kids understand the terms she used?

WRITING

ANALYZE THE STUDENT MODEL

Paragraph 1

Circle the claim in Greg's introduction. What does he do in the beginning of his introduction to get the reader's attention?

Asks questions

Paragraph 2

An example of elaboration is highlighted in the second paragraph. **Underline** the kind of business that depends on local customers and tourism.

Draw a box around each source that Greg mentions in the second paragraph. According to one source, how much money did leisure travelers spend per person per trip in 2019?

Student Model: Argumentative Essay

Greg responded to the Writing Prompt: *Write an argumentative essay about whether tourism is an important part of Colorado's economy. Read Greg's essay below.*

1   Do you like hiking in the mountains? Shopping in an outdoor walking mall? Sighting wild animals? Lots of people enjoy these and many other things in Colorado. We are lucky that so many people want to visit our state because tourism is an important part of Colorado's economy.

2   According to the text "Facts About Colorado's Economy," 86.9 million tourists visited Colorado in 2019. Why do these numbers matter? When tourists come to Colorado, they spend money. They pay for hotel rooms, restaurant meals, park admissions, and tours. All those tourist dollars help keep Colorado's economy strong. My grandparents own a restaurant in downtown Boulder. They have plenty of local customers. However they also depend on the money from tourists eating at their restaurant. The state government also depends on money from tourists. In the source "How Tourism Helps Colorado" it says, "in 2019, $1.5 billion in state and local taxes came from tourists." An infographic in "Facts About Colorado's Economy" says that 2019's leisure travelers spent an average of $516 per person per trip!

elaboration

3   Another reason that tourism is such an important part of Colorado's economy is that it provides jobs. An article for the *Colorado News* on November 20, 2019, said that Colorado's unemployment rate was the lowest it had been in forty years. All those hotels, restaurants, shops, and parks need employees. According to "Facts About Colorado's Economy," in 2019 the travel industry directly supported about 180,000 jobs. For example, my cousin works at a ski resort near Breckenridge. My uncle is a wilderness guide based in Boulder. Without the tourism industry, they would both be out of a job.

elaboration

4   Tourism makes up a big part of Colorado's economy. It provides jobs for people and helps fund our state government. With so much to see and do in Colorado, it is no wonder that we had 86.9 million visitors in 2019. Tourists have a good time in Colorado. They help keep our economy strong. It's a win for everyone.

Paragraph 3
Draw a box around the central idea of the third paragraph. What is an example of relevant evidence that supports the central idea of the paragraph?

_____

_____

_____

Underline transitional words or phrases that Greg uses to connect his ideas.

Paragraph 4
Circle the sentence that restates Greg's claim from his first paragraph. What does Greg point out in the last sentences of his conclusion?

_____

_____

_____

Apply the Rubric

With a partner, use the rubric on page 98 to discuss why Greg scored a 4 on his essay.

Analyze the Prompt

Writing Prompt

Write an argumentative essay for the school newspaper about the skills students should be learning to prepare them for jobs in the future.

Purpose, Audience, and Task Reread the writing prompt. What is your purpose for writing? My purpose is to <u>Write about the skills stedets should be learning for future jons.</u>

Who will your audience be? My audience will be <u>readers of the school newspaper</u>

What type of writing is the prompt asking for? <u>Argamentative essy</u>

Set a Purpose for Reading Sources When you are reading for information, think about what it is you want to learn about the topic. Preview the three sources in the passage set, and write what you want to learn from them below.

_____

_____

_____

Quick Tip

As you read the passage set, think about how the authors present their arguments. Ask yourself these questions:

- *How does the author feel about the topic?*
- *What reasons do they give to support their claims?*
- *What facts do the authors include to support their reasons?*
- *What examples do they provide?*

Read the following passage set.

⭐ HELP WANTED ⭐

1   Jobs help our economy. But according to national labor statistics, many of the jobs that will be in demand by 2030 have not yet been invented. Most of these new jobs will be given to people who have a college education and specialized training. Therefore, in order to keep our economy strong, we must prepare students for the future.

2   An important part of the US economy is the space industry. Advances in science and technology stimulate the economy. In 2019, NASA (National Aeronautics and Space Administration) contributed more than $64 billion to the nation's economic output. **NASA employs thousands of people throughout the United States.** The space industry requires workers who are skilled in science, math, and technology. We need to make sure that our students have the skills they need to work in the space industry. It is an important part of our economy.

3 ✱   When today's elementary students graduate from college, they will need jobs. According to the World Economic Forum, 65 percent of those students will have jobs that don't exist right now. Let's start figuring out how we can help students get the skills they need to succeed in the future.

NASA/Sandy Joseph and Tim Terry

ARGUMENTATIVE ESSAY

FIND TEXT EVIDENCE 🔍

Paragraph 1
Circle the claim. What will most people in the future need to get a job?

college education
specialized training

Paragraph 2
Read the technique of elaboration that has been highlighted for you. Why is the space industry important?

Employs thousands of people

Underline the skills needed to work in the space industry.

Paragraph 3
What kinds of jobs will 65 percent of today's elementary students be working at in the future?

jobs that don't exist

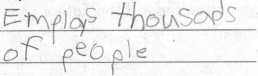 **Take Notes** Paraphrase the author's claim and give examples of supporting details.

FIND TEXT EVIDENCE

Paragraph 4

Draw a box around the claim. What will workers have to do by 2030?

_____

_____

Paragraph 5

Circle the details that tell where the five skills are being taught. Read the highlighted example of elaboration. How does this quotation support the author's claim?

_____

_____

_____

List of Skills

Read the list. Where might you learn teamwork skills?

_____

Take Notes Paraphrase the author's claim and give examples of supporting details.

Skills for the Future

4   By the year 2030, workers will have to learn new skills to keep their jobs. Many people want to know what these new skills are and teach them to students now. However, we're already teaching our students the skills they need.

5   A survey asked business leaders what skills students will need when they graduate. The results of the survey show five skills that workers will need in the future. These skills are listed below. The good news is that these skills are already being taught in the classroom and on the playing field. **As the head of one university said, "Educators have always found new ways of training the next generation of students for the jobs of the future. This generation will be no different."**

SKILLS FOR THE FUTURE

1 Critical Thinking and Problem Solving

2 Teamwork Skills

3 Flexible Thinking

4 Initiative

5 Effective Writing and Communication Skills

Look to the future

6   A new study by the McKinsey Global Institute says almost 800 million jobs will disappear in the next fifteen years. The reason? Robots and machines will do the work instead of people. However, one job that will never disappear is being an entrepreneur. In the future, what we will really need are social entrepreneurs.

7   Social entrepreneurs start businesses to help improve the lives of others. At the same time, they make a profit, too. Some of these businesses help relieve poverty and hunger. Others work on improving education or the environment.

8   One entrepreneur combined two passions to form a business. A love of the environment and a science degree led to a business in cleaning products. This entrepreneur was determined to create cleaning products that do not contain toxins. Toxic chemicals are harmful to people and the environment. This business addresses a social and environmental problem. And it offers solutions.

9   What kinds of skills do you need to become a social entrepreneur? You need ideas, creativity, initiative, and a desire to help others. Some high schools and universities have social entrepreneur programs. These programs help students develop their ideas. It is never too early to think about starting a business to help others.

Ekaterina Markelova/Shutterstock

ARGUMENTATIVE ESSAY

FIND TEXT EVIDENCE

Paragraph 6
What does the author think will be needed in the future?
social entrepreneurs

Paragraph 7
Underline the details that tell what a social entrepreneur is.

Paragraph 8
What is an example of how the cleaning products company helps others?

cleaning produds w/out toxins

Paragraph 9
Circle the skills needed to become a social entrepreneur. What resources can help students become social entrepreneurs?

Take Notes Paraphrase the author's claim and give examples of supporting details.

My Goal I can synthesize information from three sources.

TAKE NOTES

Read the writing prompt below. Write your claim. Then use the three sources, your notes, and the graphic organizer to plan a response.

Writing Prompt *Write an argumentative essay for the school newspaper about the skills students should be learning to prepare them for jobs in the future.*

Synthesize Information

Review the sources. Think about the facts and ideas that agree with your claim. Then think about what you know about the topic. Discuss your ideas with a partner.

Plan: Organize Ideas

Claim	Reasons
There are a variety of skills students should be learning to prepare them for jobs in the future.	The kinds of skills that are needed are . . .

Valentain Jevee/Shutterstock

Relevant Evidence

Source 1	Source 2	Source 3

Draft: Strong Introduction

Write an Effective Introduction Your introduction should grab your reader's attention and clearly state, or make, your claim. Read the introduction below from Greg's argumentative essay on page 100. The writer's claim is highlighted.

> Do you like hiking in the mountains? Shopping in an outdoor walking mall? Sighting wild animals? Lots of people enjoy these and many other things in Colorado. **We are lucky that so many people want to visit our state because tourism is an important part of Colorado's economy.**

Writers use questions in their writing to grab the reader's attention. Adjectives such as *lucky* and *important* emphasize the writer's feelings about the topic. The writer's claim is clearly stated. Readers know that the essay will be about why tourism is important to Colorado's economy. Use the claim above as a model to write an introduction for your essay.

_____

_____

_____

_____

Draft Use your graphic organizer and introduction above to write your draft in your writer's notebook. Before you start writing, review the rubric on page 98. Remember to indent each paragraph.

Grammar Connections

Write different kinds of sentences to strengthen your essay. For example, ask a question at the beginning of a paragraph: *Do you like hiking in the mountains?* Or add an exclamation: *I love going there!* Try beginning a sentence with a verb: *Sighting wild animals . . .*

If your sentences are all the same length, combine some sentences to make a compound sentence. Or make a longer sentence shorter.

CHECK IN 1 2 3 4

Revise: Peer Conferences

Review a Draft Listen actively to your partner. Take notes about what you liked and what was difficult to follow. Begin by telling what you liked. Use these sentence starters.

Your claim was persuasive because . . .
What did you mean by . . .
I think adding more facts can help to . . .

After you give each other feedback, reflect on the peer conference. How can you use the guidance from your partner to help improve your writing?

_____

_____

Revision Use the Revising Checklist to help you figure out what text you may need to move, elaborate on, or delete. After you finish writing your final draft, use the full rubric on pages 236–239 to score your essay.

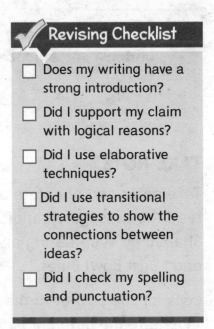

✔ **Revising Checklist**

☐ Does my writing have a strong introduction?

☐ Did I support my claim with logical reasons?

☐ Did I use elaborative techniques?

☐ Did I use transitional strategies to show the connections between ideas?

☐ Did I check my spelling and punctuation?

Turn to page 85. Fill in the bars to show what you learned.

My Score			
Purpose, Focus, & Organization (4 pts)	Evidence & Elaboration (4 pts)	Conventions (2 pts)	Total (10 pts)

My Goal I can read and understand science texts.

TAKE NOTES

Take notes and annotate as you read the passages "Landforms Shaped by Weathering and Erosion" and "Dust Bowl Blues."

Look for the answer to the question: *What are the different factors that can cause landforms to change?*

_____

_____

_____

_____

_____

_____

_____

_____

PASSAGE 1

EXPOSITORY TEXT

Landforms Shaped by
WEATHERING AND EROSION

In Palo Duro Canyon, Texas, bands of red, brown, and white show years of history. But how did this canyon take shape? The answer is weathering and erosion.

Palo Duro Canyon

Weathering

Weathering is the slow process of breaking down rocks into smaller pieces. Rain, wind, ice, and flowing water are some of the causes. Have you ever noticed the ragged sections of mountains? They are caused by weathering.

Erosion

In contrast, erosion is the moving of rocks and soil by wind, water, gravity, or ice to another place. Gravity moves rocks downhill. Rain carries rock particles into rivers. Then the moving water carries the small pieces of rock and soil downhill. The particles in water can carve rocks into valleys. But it takes a very long time.

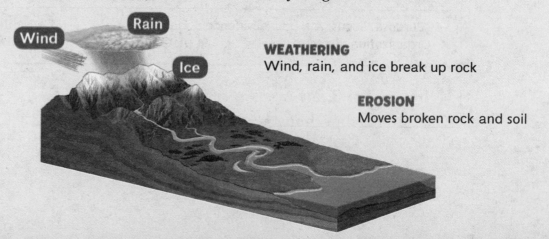

Wind Rain Ice

WEATHERING
Wind, rain, and ice break up rock

EROSION
Moves broken rock and soil

(t)Zack Frank/Shutterstock.com

Wind and ice cause erosion, too. A lot of energy is needed to move rocks and soil particles by wind. In the early 1930s, overfarming and drought caused farms in the Great Plains to turn to dust. Fierce winds eroded this dry soil and sometimes carried it many states away. During these wind storms, the sky would turn black from the dust. They were called "black blizzards." Powerful winds can also break down large rocks into smaller pieces. Then water can carry away those pieces. The type of rock and the intensity of the wind affect the rate at which erosion occurs. Hard rocks take longer to erode than softer rocks. Yet no rock is safe from erosion. Ice can erode landforms too. Ice and large sheets of ice called *glaciers* move rocks from the ground. A glacier scratches, breaks, or carries away the things in its path.

PASSAGE
2 NARRATIVE NONFICTION
DUST BOWL Blues

Have you ever seen a blizzard? All that snow blinding everything in its path? Now imagine instead of snow, heavy winds are blowing tons of dust everywhere. During the Great Depression, people called these dust storms "black blizzards." In 1932, there were fourteen of them. A year later, there were almost forty. What caused these dust storms? Why did the Great Plains—including parts of Oklahoma, Texas, Kansas, Colorado, and New Mexico—become known as the "Dust Bowl"?

TAKE NOTES

TAKE NOTES

_____

_____

_____

_____

_____

_____

_____

_____

_____

_____

_____

_____

_____

_____

_____

_____

_____

"It Turned My Farm into a Pile of Sand"

During the 1910s and 1920s, rising wheat prices and government policies created a land boom. Homesteaders in the Great Plains ripped up grasslands to plant wheat. The result was the loss of root support for holding the soil together. Grass and trees are like anchors for topsoil. By the 1930s, the depleted farms met a new foe: the worst drought in US history. The once waving wheat fields turned to dust.

"Dusty Old Dust"

Then the storms began. Heavy winds caused soil erosion. Tons of dust blew into the once blue sky, creating complete darkness. Businesses and schools closed. People wore gauze masks to keep the sand out of their eyes, nose, and mouth. Many people migrated to California and other western states to work on farms. But it became challenging in those states to house the migrants.

"Dust Can't Kill Me"

In 1935, the US government created the Soil Conservation Service. The service advised farmers to plant trees and change their farming techniques. Farmers began to rotate crops and rest the land. These conservation efforts worked. By 1938, the dust storm numbers were reduced by half.

Finally, it rained heavily in 1939, ending the drought. By 1941, most of the destruction was repaired. But generations of people in the Great Plains will never forget those Dust Bowl days.

(bkg)MCT/Tribune News Service/Getty Images; (inset) U.S. Department of Agriculture

COMPARE THE PASSAGES

Review your notes from both passages. Then create a Venn diagram like the one below. Use your notes and the diagram to record how the information in the two passages is alike and different.

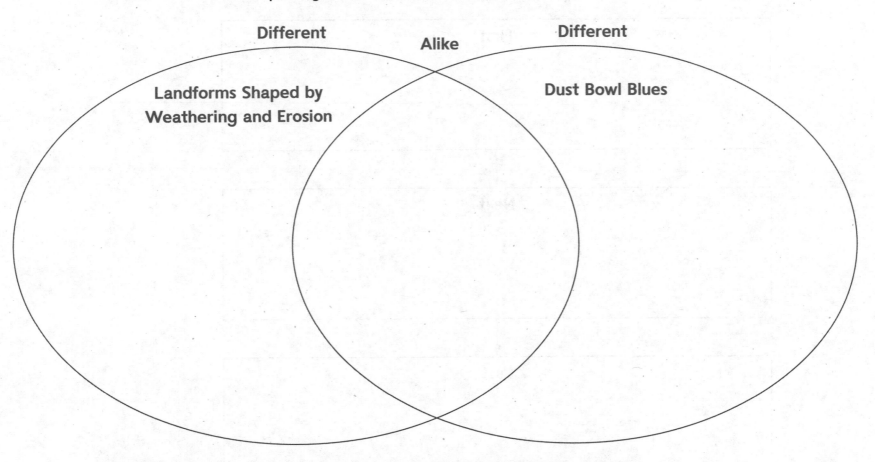

Different | Alike | Different

Landforms Shaped by Weathering and Erosion

Dust Bowl Blues

Synthesize Information

Think about both texts. In your reader's notebook, write an answer to these questions: How does weather affect landforms? What else can affect landforms?

CHECK IN ▷ 1 ▷ 2 ▷ 3 ▷ 4

CHRONOLOGY

Reread "Dust Bowl Blues," and think about the chronology, or time order, that led to the Dust Bowl. Then complete the chronology chart below.

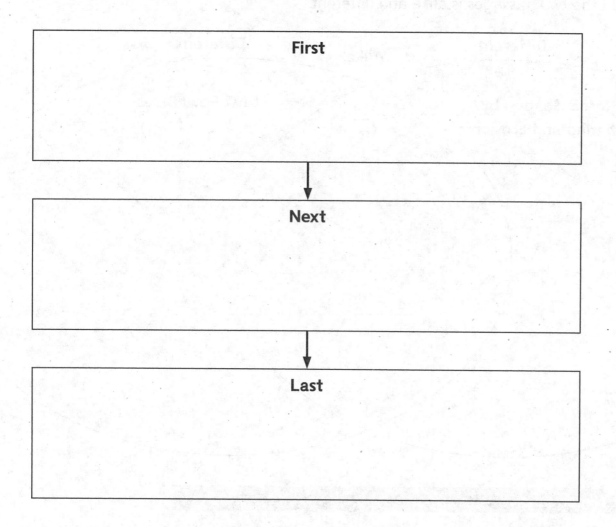

First

Next

Last

WRITE A SCIENTIFIC ARTICLE

Imagine you work for the Soil Conservation Service in 1935. You have been asked to write an article explaining why the Dust Bowl occurred and how it could be prevented from happening again. Use facts from "Dust Bowl Blues" and the chronology chart you completed on page 114 to write the article.

TAKE NOTES

Take notes and annotate as you read the passage "Developing a Nation's Economy."

Look for the answer to the question: *How did Elizabeth Keckly, An Wang, and Rebecca Lukens help the economy to grow?*

_____

_____

_____

_____

_____

_____

_____

_____

_____

PASSAGE 1

BIOGRAPHY

Developing *a Nation's* Economy

Elizabeth Keckly, An Wang, and Rebecca Lukens each played a unique role in helping parts of the United States economy to grow.

Elizabeth Keckly

When Elizabeth Keckly was young, she did not imagine that she would one day design gowns for a First Lady of the United States. Keckly was born into slavery in 1818. While in St. Louis, Missouri, the enslaved Keckly became a skilled seamstress. Many women in St. Louis bought her dresses, and she became well known.

Keckly was determined that she and her son become free. She later said she "could not stay silent." She worked hard and saved money. In 1855 she used those savings to buy freedom for them both.

Keckly moved to Washington, D.C., and worked for a dressmaker. Then she began designing dresses herself. Dressmaking paid well. Keckly's dresses became famous for their wonderful fit and design.

One of Keckly's customers introduced her to Mary Todd Lincoln, the wife of Abraham Lincoln, who was about to become the president of the United States. Mrs. Lincoln loved the dress Keckly made for her and asked her to make more. The two became friends.

Keckly was smart in business. Her business employed 20 seamstresses and provided many opportunities for other African American women. "I have experienced many ups and downs," she wrote, "but still am stout of heart."

AN WANG

An Wang was born in Shanghai, China. As a child he was good at mathematics and science. At university, he studied electrical engineering from American textbooks. This was not a problem for him, since he started learning English when he was four.

During World War II, Wang helped provide radios to Chinese troops. At one point he improvised radios out of found parts. When the war was nearly over, Wang took a competitive test and was chosen to study in the United States. He was accepted to Harvard, even though it was hard to get into this university. He wrote that he could not imagine "that there were things I could not or should not attempt to accomplish."

Once he had his degree, Wang took a job at the Harvard Computation Laboratory because it was nearby. It was a good decision. It was Wang's work in computers that made him famous!

At that time, in 1948, electrical computers did not store information well. Within a few months of work, Wang had an idea that led to the invention of magnetic core memory. It kept data even when a computer lost power.

Wang's work allowed electric computers to do many important jobs. The US Navy used such computers to track aircraft. Similar computers helped guide NASA's Apollo missions to the Moon.

In 1955, Wang sold his core memory patent and started his own business. It was one of the first companies to make desktop calculators. It also created early office computers. His company introduced people to new technologies and, like Wang himself, became world-famous. Wang was inducted into the National Inventors Hall of Fame in 1988.

TAKE NOTES

TAKE NOTES

Rebecca Lukens

Rebecca Lukens learned about the making of iron when she was a child in Pennsylvania. Her family owned Brandywine Iron Works, and her father taught her the business. When Lukens married in 1813, her husband took over the business. After her husband's death in 1825, she took over the business and became one of America's first female ironmasters. She was up for the challenge.

At this time, the United States was a young country with a growing economy. Technologies were changing quickly. Brandywine Iron Works began creating parts for the then brand-new steam engines. It became well known for producing a special plate for iron-hulled steamships.

In 1837, the US economy hit a terrible time that lasted many years. Businesses and banks closed. Many people lost their jobs. There was little business for iron works companies.

However, Lukens was both a smart business person and a caring employer. Her family had taught her the importance of community and fair treatment. Even in difficult years, Lukens found ways to keep her employees working. She kept making high-quality products. Because of her wise management, Brandywine Iron Works made it through.

Lukens helped support inventions such as the steam engine, which changed life across the United States. She also proved that taking care of employees and embracing new technologies can lead to great success.

George Sheldon/Alamy Stock Photo

DETERMINING CAUSE AND EFFECT

Reread the passage "Developing a Nation's Economy." Then complete the cause-and-effect chart below.

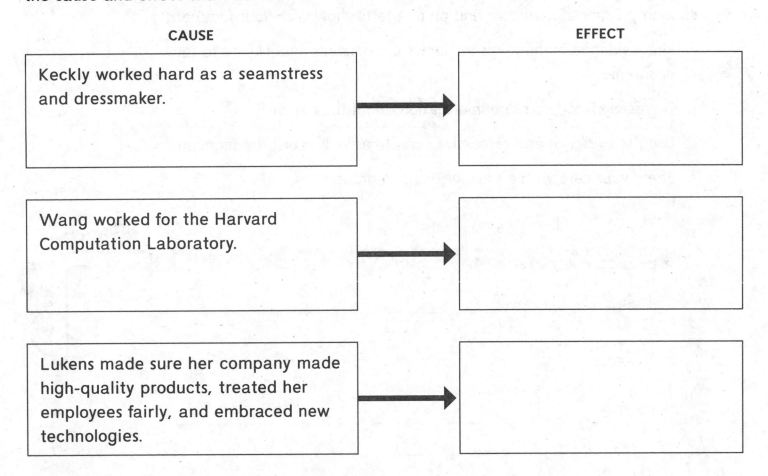

CAUSE

EFFECT

Keckly worked hard as a seamstress and dressmaker.

Wang worked for the Harvard Computation Laboratory.

Lukens made sure her company made high-quality products, treated her employees fairly, and embraced new technologies.

Synthesize Information

Think about the texts. How did these people affect the US economy, as well as the lives of others? How did this help develop economies? Write your ideas in your reader's notebook.

CHECK IN   1   2   3   4

CONNECT TO CONTENT

CREATE A FACT CARD

Choose one of the people you read about in "Developing a Nation's Economy." Create a fact card with that person's contributions to the economy. Draw a picture or find an image to show with your fact card.

- Find evidence in the text that shows the person's importance to the economy.

- Do research to find more information about the person.

- Use the evidence and research to create an online or print fact card.

- Share your card with a partner or small group.

The person I chose is _____

FACT 1: _____

_____

FACT 2: _____

_____

FACT 3: _____

Reflect on Your Learning

Talk About It Reflect on what you learned in this unit. Then talk with a partner about how you did.

I am really proud of how I can _____

_____

_____

_____

_____

Something I need to work more on is _____

_____

_____

_____

_____

My Goal Set a goal for Unit 2. In your reader's notebook, write about what you can do to get there.

> Share a goal you have with a partner.

Build Knowledge

? Essential Question

What helps an animal survive?

Build Vocabulary

Write new words you learned about what helps animals survive.
Draw lines and circles for the words you write.

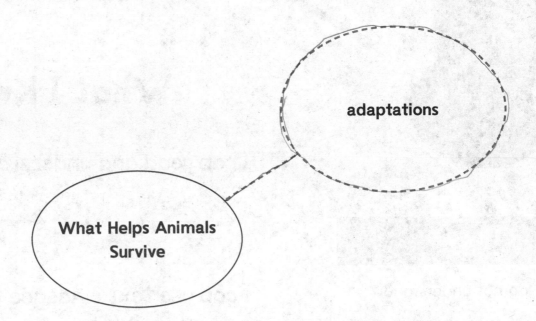

adaptations

What Helps Animals
Survive

Go online to **my.mheducation.com** and read the "Hidden in Plain Sight" Blast.
How does camouflage help animals survive in their environment? Blast back
your response.

Think about what you already know. Wherever you are is okay. Fill in the bars.

What I Know Now

Key
1 = I do not understand.
2 = I understand but need more practice.
3 = I understand.
4 = I understand and can teach someone.

I can read and understand expository text.

1 > 2 > 3 > 4

I can use text evidence to respond to expository text.

1 > 2 > 3 > 4

I know what helps an animal survive.

1 > 2 > 3 > 4

 **STOP** You will come back to the next page later.

What I Learned

I can read and understand expository text.

1 2 3 4

I can use text evidence to respond to expository text.

1 2 3 4

I know what helps an animal survive.

1 2 3 4

My Goal I can read and understand expository text.

TAKE NOTES

As you read, make note of interesting words and important information.

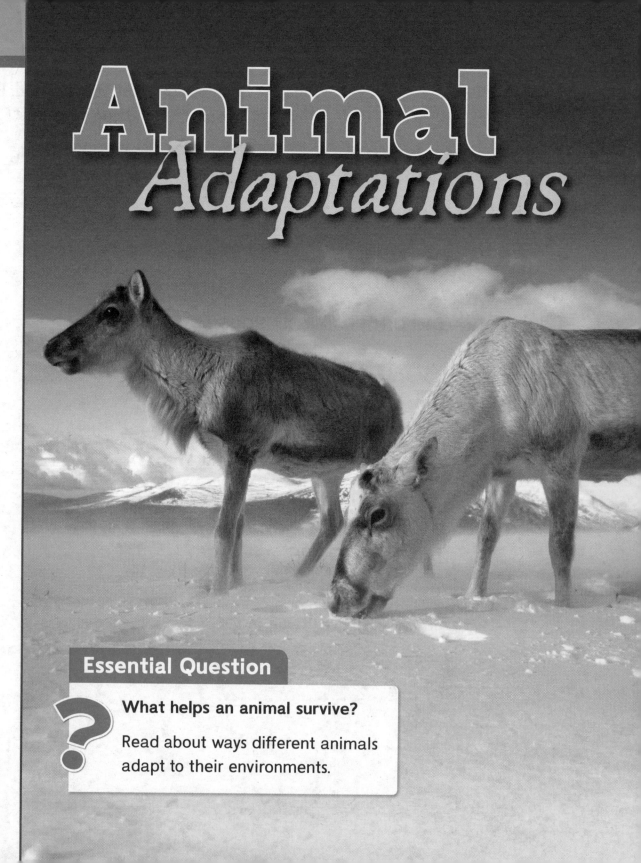

Animal Adaptations

Essential Question

What helps an animal survive?

Read about ways different animals adapt to their environments.

What would you do if you saw a skunk raise its tail? If you knew anything about skunks, you would run in the opposite direction! Skunks have a built-in survival system. They can blast a **predator** with a horrible-smelling spray produced by the glands under their tails.

The special ways that animals have to survive are called adaptations. These include physical traits such as the skunk's spray and animals with bright colors and markings that warn predators that they are **poisonous**. Some animals can sense the smallest **vibrations** in the ground. Others hear sounds from miles away. An adaptation can also be a behavioral trait. An example of a behavioral trait would be birds that migrate south every winter to avoid harsh temperatures.

When a skunk turns and sprays a predator, the foul-smelling mist can travel up to 10 feet.

Staying Warm

Brrrr! Imagine living in a place where the average annual temperature is an **extraordinary** 10° to 20°F. Welcome to the Arctic tundra of Alaska, Canada, Greenland, and Russia, home of the caribou. To stay warm, caribou have two layers of fur and a thick layer of fat. They also have compact bodies. Only 4 or 5 feet long, caribou can weigh over 500 pounds.

The tip of the caribou's nose and mouth is called a muzzle. It is covered in short hair. This hair helps to warm the air before they inhale it into their lungs. It also helps to keep them warm as they push snow aside to find food.

(bkgd) blickwinkel/Alamy Stock Photo; (r) Comstock/Getty Images

FIND TEXT EVIDENCE

Read

Paragraphs 1–2
Central Idea and Details
Circle the sentence that states the central idea in paragraph 2.
Underline the details about physical traits that help animals to survive.

Paragraphs 3–4
Summarize

Summarize the caribou's physical adaptations on these lines.

_____

_____

_____

_____

Reread

Author's Craft

How do the author's details about the caribou help you to make an inference about what animals need to survive in the Arctic tundra?

Read

Paragraph 1

Photograph and Caption

Underline the details in the text that support the photo and caption.

Prefixes

The prefix *un-* means "not." **Circle** the word that has the *un-* prefix. Write the word's meaning below.

_____

Paragraph 2

Summarize

Write the most important information to summarize the adaptations of phasmids.

_____

_____

_____

Reread

Author's Craft

How does the author use the photo and caption to help you understand the phasmid's adaptation?

Finding Food

Every day, a caribou eats over six pounds of lichen! Caribou have unusual stomachs. The stomach's four chambers are designed to digest lichen. It is one of the few foods they can find in the winter. Even so, caribou still have a tough time in the coldest part of winter when their food sources decline. That's why they travel from the tundra to a large forest area, where food is easier to find. When the melting snow **dribbles** into streams, they know that it is time to return up north.

Lichen can grow in extreme temperatures.

Insects in Disguise

Look closely at the photo of the tree branch. Can you spot the insect? It is a phasmid. Some phasmids are known as leaf insects, or walking sticks. Phasmids look like leaves or twigs. These insects can change colors to really blend in with their surroundings. In this way, they are **camouflaged** from predators. It's as if they disappear from sight! These insects are nocturnal, which means that they are active at night. This is another adaptation that helps them avoid predators. It's hard to spot these insects in daylight, let alone at night.

This phasmid is called a walking stick because it looks like a stick with legs.

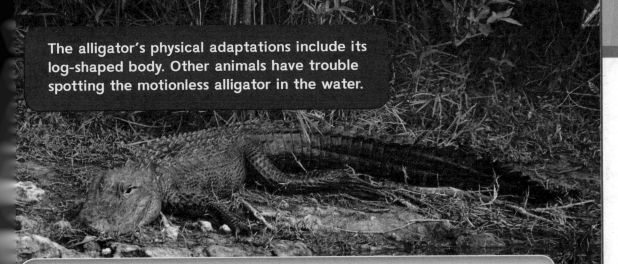

The alligator's physical adaptations include its log-shaped body. Other animals have trouble spotting the motionless alligator in the water.

Water, Please!

In Florida's vast Everglades ecosystem, the dry season is brutal for many plants and animals. Alligators have found a way to survive these dry conditions in the freshwater marshes. They use their feet and snouts to clear dirt from holes in the limestone bedrock. When the ground dries up, the alligators can drink from their water holes.

Other species benefit from these water holes, too. Plants grow there. Other animals find water to survive the dry season. However, the animals that visit alligator holes become easy **prey**. The normally motionless alligator may **pounce** on them without warning. But luckily, alligators eat only a few times each month. Many animals take their chances and revisit the alligator hole when they need water. In the end, it's all about survival!

Summarize

Use your notes, the headings, and the photographs to help you summarize "Animal Adaptations."

EXPOSITORY TEXT

FIND TEXT EVIDENCE

Read

Headings

Why is "Water, Please!" a good heading for this section?

_____

_____

_____

Central Idea and Details

Underline all the details in the caption and text about adaptations that help an alligator to survive.

Reread

Author's Craft

The author describes how alligators dig water holes to survive the dry season. How does that description show that one animal's adaptation helps and hurts other animals?

Vocabulary

Use the example sentences to talk with a partner about each word. Then answer the questions.

camouflaged

The green frog is **camouflaged** because it blends in with the grass.

What other animals are camouflaged in their environment?

_____

_____

_____

dribbles

Water **dribbles** down from the leaky roof.

What is something else that dribbles?

_____

_____

extraordinary

Schools were closed because of the **extraordinary** amount of snow in town!

What is an antonym for _extraordinary_?

_____

_____

poisonous

Some wild mushrooms are **poisonous** and can make you sick.

What other things are poisonous?

_____

_____

pounce

My cat loves to **pounce** on her toy mouse.

What other animals pounce?

_____

_____

Build Your Word List Pick one of the interesting words you noted on page 126 and look up its meaning in a print or digital dictionary. Pronounce the word and count the syllables. Write one statement and one question using the word. Share your two sentences with a partner.

predator

An owl is a **predator** that hunts for food at night.

What other animal is a predator?

_____

_____

prey

A mouse is **prey** for owls and other predators.

What do you think would be prey for a shark?

_____

_____

vibrations

When you strum on the strings of a guitar, you cause **vibrations** because the strings move back and forth quickly.

What else can make vibrations?

_____

_____

Prefixes

As you read, you may come across a word that you don't know. Look for word parts such as prefixes. A prefix is added to the beginning of a word and changes its meaning. Here are some common prefixes.

un- means "not"
re- means "again"
dis- means "opposite of"

FIND TEXT EVIDENCE

When I read the section "Staying Warm" on page 127 in "Animal Adaptations," I see the word extraordinary. *First, I look at the separate word parts. I know that* extra *is a prefix that changes the meaning of* ordinary. *The prefix* extra *means "beyond."*

Imagine living in a place where the average annual temperature is an **extraordinary** 10° to 20°F.

Your Turn Use prefixes and context clues to figure out the meanings of the following words.

disappear, page 128_____

revisit, page 129_____

CHECK IN ⟩ 1 ⟩ 2 ⟩ 3 ⟩ 4 ⟩

Summarize

When you summarize, you use your own words to tell the most important ideas or information. This helps you to better understand and remember what you have learned.

FIND TEXT EVIDENCE

Reread the section "Insects in Disguise" on page 128. Identify the most important information to summarize the section.

Page 128

Insects in Disguise

Some phasmids are known as leaf insects, or walking sticks. Phasmids look like leaves or twigs. These insects can change colors to really blend in with their surroundings. In this way, they are **camouflaged** from predators. It's as if they disappear from sight! These insects are nocturnal, which means that they are active at night. This is another adaptation that helps them avoid predators. It's hard to spot these insects in daylight, let alone at night.

Phasmids are insects that can camouflage themselves to avoid predators. In addition, phasmids are nocturnal, which makes them difficult for predators to spot.

COLLABORATE

Your Turn Reread "Water, Please!" on page 129 and summarize the section.

____

____

____

Quick Tip

Remember that summaries include only the most important information from a text. To summarize a text, you can ask *who, what, where, when, why,* and *how* questions.

Use these sentence starters.

- *The text is about . . .*
- *One important detail is . . .*
- *Another important detail is . . .*

CHECK IN 1 2 3 4

Photographs, Captions, and Headings

"Animal Adaptations" is an expository, or informational, text. Expository texts give facts and information about a topic. They may include text features such as **photographs, captions,** and **headings.**

FIND TEXT EVIDENCE

I can tell "Animal Adaptations" is an expository text because it gives me facts about how different animals have adapted. I see that each section has a heading. The text also includes photographs and captions.

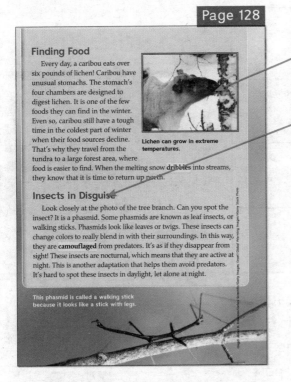

Page 128

Finding Food

Every day, a caribou eats over six pounds of lichen! Caribou have unusual stomachs. The stomach's four chambers are designed to digest lichen. It is one of the few foods they can find in the winter. Even so, caribou still have a tough time in the coldest part of winter when their food sources decline. That's why they travel from the tundra to a large forest area, where food is easier to find. When the melting snow **dribbles** into streams, they know that it is time to return up north.

Lichen can grow in extreme temperatures.

Insects in Disguise

Look closely at the photo of the tree branch. Can you spot the insect? It is a phasmid. Some phasmids are known as leaf insects, or walking sticks. Phasmids look like leaves or twigs. These insects can change colors to really blend in with their surroundings. In this way, they are **camouflaged** from predators. It's as if they disappear from sight! These insects are nocturnal, which means that they are active at night. This is another adaptation that helps them avoid predators. It's hard to spot these insects in daylight, let alone at night.

This phasmid is called a walking stick because it looks like a stick with legs.

Photographs and Captions

Photographs illustrate what is in the text. Captions provide additional information.

Headings

Headings tell what a section of text is mostly about.

COLLABORATE

Your Turn Find and list two text features in "Animal Adaptations." Tell your partner what information you learned from each of these features.

_____

_____

_____

CHECK IN 1 2 3 4

Central Idea and Relevant Details

A topic is the subject of the text. The central idea is the most important point that the author is making about the topic. Relevant details tell more about the topic and support the central idea.

🔍 FIND TEXT EVIDENCE

To find the central idea of "Staying Warm" on page 127, first I'll think about the topic. The topic is how caribou stay warm. Then I'll look for details that tell more about, or are relevant to, the topic. Next I will evaluate what the details have in common. I'll use that information to identify the central idea.

Quick Tip

A topic is general. A central idea is specific.
Topic: Growing Tulips
Central Idea: It is easy to grow tulips.

Sometimes authors directly state a central idea. To better understand the stated idea, look for details that give more information and support the idea.

Central Idea
Caribou adaptations help the animal to survive the cold.
Detail
Caribou have two layers of fur.
Detail
Caribou have a thick layer of fat.
Detail
Short hair on their muzzles warms the air that they inhale.

Your Turn Reread the section "Insects in Disguise" on page 128. Find the relevant details and list them in the graphic organizer on page 135. Use these details to figure out the central idea. Explain to your partner how the details support the central idea.

Global Warming Images/Alamy Stock Photo

CHECK IN 〉1〉2〉3〉4〉

Central Idea
Detail
Detail
Detail

Respond to Reading

COLLABORATE Discuss the prompt below. Use your notes and text evidence to support your response.

> Why are adaptations important? Use evidence from the text to support your response.
>
> _____
>
> _____
>
> _____
>
> _____
>
> _____
>
> _____
>
> _____
>
> _____
>
> _____
>
> _____
>
> _____
>
> _____

Quick Tip

Use these sentence starters to discuss the text and organize your ideas.

- *An example of an adaptation is . . .*
- *This adaptation is important because . . .*
- *Another kind of adaptation is . . .*

Grammar Connections

Check to make sure you have no run-on sentences.

Run-on sentence: *Alligators make water holes these holes can help other species.*

Correct sentence: *Alligators make water holes. These holes can help other species.*

CHECK IN   1 〉 2 〉 3 〉 4 〉

Animal Survival

COLLABORATE

Insects go through a series of physical changes, called a life cycle, that are important to their survival. Follow the research process to write a report that compares the life cycles of two insects in your area. Include a life-cycle diagram for each insect to show the changes, or stages, it goes through in its lifetime. Work with a partner.

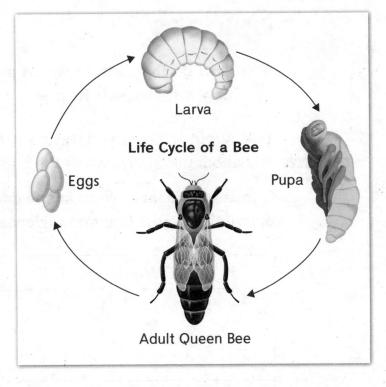

Life Cycle of a Bee

Larva

Eggs

Pupa

Adult Queen Bee

Step 1 **Set a Goal** Brainstorm a list of local insects that you would like to know more about. Then choose two insects to study.

Step 2 **Identify Sources** Use books, magazines, and websites to find information about your insects.

Step 3 **Find and Record Information** Find information in your sources and take notes. Look for images you may want to include. Keep track of your sources so that you can cite them in your report.

The diagram above shows the life cycle of a honeybee. What happens to an egg? Write your answer here.

_____

_____

_____

_____

Step 4 **Organize and Synthesize Information** Create a rough sketch of each life-cycle diagram. Decide what images and captions you will use. How are the two cycles alike or different? Make a compare-and-contrast chart to organize your ideas.

Step 5 **Create and Present** Create a final copy of the life-cycle diagrams. Use your chart to write a paragraph comparing the two life cycles. Decide how to present your work to the class.

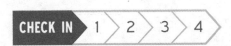
CHECK IN 1 2 3 4

Spiders

 How do the author's words and phrases help you visualize how a spider eats its prey?

Literature Anthology: pages 90–105

 Talk About It Reread **Literature Anthology** page 94. With a partner, talk about descriptive words the author uses for how the spider eats.

Cite Text Evidence What image does the author create with these descriptive words? Cite text evidence from the paragraph.

 Synthesize Information

Combine what you already know about adaptations. Think about the adaptations a spider has and how they help it to survive. Compare the ways a spider gets and eats food with the ways other animals you have learned about get and eat food.

Words	What I Visualize

Write The author helps me visualize how a spider eats its prey by _____

_____

_____

How does the author help you understand his perspective, or feelings, about how a spider uses its senses?

 Talk About It Reread page 98 of the **Literature Anthology**. Turn to your partner and talk about the way the author describes the body parts of a spider that sense things.

Cite Text Evidence What evidence does the author give that helps you understand his feelings about the spider? Write text evidence and explain the author's feelings, or perspective.

Quick Tip

You can use these sentence starters when you talk about the author's perspective about the spider's senses.

- *The author thinks the spider's senses are . . .*

- *One of the reasons he feels this way is . . .*

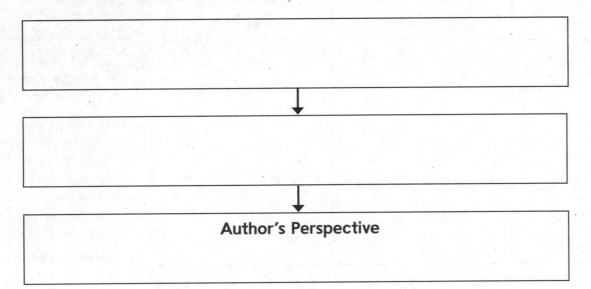

Author's Perspective

Write I know how the author feels about the spider's senses because

_____

_____

_____

CHECK IN 1 2 3 4

? **How do the text features help you understand more about orb web spiders?**

COLLABORATE

Talk About It Reread page 105 of the **Literature Anthology**. Look at the photograph on page 104 and read the caption that goes with it. Turn to your partner and talk about what new information you learned.

Cite Text Evidence What details in the text features give you more information about orb web spiders? Write text evidence in the chart.

Text Evidence	Photograph	Caption

Write The author uses text features to _____

_____

_____

Quick Tip

When you look at the text features, connect the caption with what you see in the photograph. Use these sentence starters.

- *In the photo, I see . . .*
- *When I read the caption, I learn . . .*
- *The caption connects to the photo because . . .*

Make Inferences

Orb web spiders make enough silk to produce large spiderwebs. Most spiders make their webs at night. Why do you think most spiders make their webs at night?

CHECK IN ⟩ 1 ⟩ 2 ⟩ 3 ⟩ 4 ⟩

Respond to Reading

COLLABORATE Discuss the prompt below. Use your notes and text evidence to support your response.

Do you agree with the author's perspective on spiders? Explain using evidence from the text.

_____

_____

_____

_____

_____

_____

_____

_____

_____

_____

_____

_____

Quick Tip

Use these sentence starters to discuss the text and organize your text evidence.

- *The author thinks that . . .*
- *I know the author's perspective on spiders because . . .*
- *I agree/disagree that . . .*

CHECK IN 1 2 3 4

Ingram Publishing/SuperStock

Anansi and the Birds

Literature Anthology: pages 108–109

1   Anansi always welcomed a challenge. His attempts to fool merchants out of their riches and lions from their jungle thrones made for exciting adventures. Today he would show those haughty birds that he could fly with the best of them.

2   He begged a feather from every bird he could find to create his own pair of wings, and then he began to practice flying. Anansi's wings camouflaged him well, and he looked just like a bird.

3   "Hoot!" the old owl chided under the moon. "A spider is not meant for the sky. Why do you try to be something you are not?"

4   "Mind your business, owl," Anansi replied angrily. "You are a predator, so go hunt some mice!"

5   Anansi followed the birds to their feast on top of a mountain peak. He helped himself to their fare, shoving birds aside to get his fill. When he was full, he fell into a deep sleep.

Reread paragraphs 1 and 2. **Circle** text evidence in paragraph 1 that tells you about Anansi's character.

COLLABORATE

Reread paragraphs 3 and 4. Talk with a partner about the relationship between Anansi and the old owl. **Underline** the dialogue that helps you understand how the owl feels about what Anansi is doing.

Then reread paragraph 5. How does the author hint that something unpleasant might happen to Anansi? **Draw a box** around the clue. Write it here:

_____

_____

6   Angrily, the birds took back the feathers from his wings and then left, all except for one crow. When Anansi awoke, he realized what had happened and begged the crow to help him get down the mountain.

7   "Of course," the crow replied slyly as he shoved Anansi over a cliff.

8   "Aaaayeeee!" shouted Anansi. Unable to fly, he tumbled helplessly through the air.

9   The old owl appeared before him, asking, "Why didn't you listen, Anansi? You are not a bird!"

10   "Please help me, owl!" pleaded Anansi.

11   The owl urged Anansi, "Push in your belly!" When he did, threads of silk shot out behind him. The owl caught them and tied them to a high branch. Dangling by threads, Anansi realized the owl was right. From that day on, he stuck to spinning webs instead of trying to be something he was not.

Reread paragraphs 6–9. **Circle** the words and phrases that describe how the birds feel about Anansi, and what they did.

COLLABORATE

With a partner, reread paragraphs 10 and 11. Talk about how the owl helps Anansi.

Then **underline** the sentence that tells how the spider feels about the owl now. Write the text evidence here:

_____

? How does the author help you understand how the characters' traits affect the story?

COLLABORATE

Talk About It Reread the excerpt on page 142. Talk about the characters' actions and feelings. What do these thoughts and actions reveal about the characters' traits? How do these traits affect the story?

Cite Text Evidence What details help you understand each character's traits? Record text evidence. How do the traits affect the story?

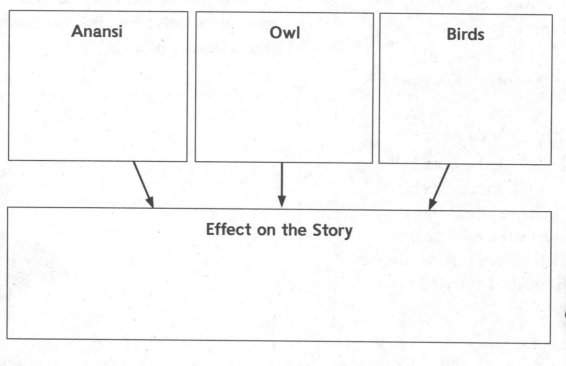

Anansi	Owl	Birds

Effect on the Story

Write The author helps me understand how the characters' traits affect the story by _____

_____

_____

Make Inferences

What the characters say and do gives the reader clues about how a character may act in the future. This is making an inference. What do you think the relationship between Anansi and the birds will be like in the future?

CHECK IN 1 2 3 4

Character Development

Characters in fiction develop, or change, during a story. These changes cause events that contribute to, or affect, the plot.

🔍 FIND TEXT EVIDENCE

In the beginning of the story, Anansi believes he can fly just as well as the birds. When the old owl tells Anansi that spiders can't fly, Anansi gets angry. He doesn't want to listen to the owl. He thinks he can do whatever he wants.

> "Mind your business, owl," Anansi replied angrily. "You are a predator, so go hunt some mice!"

Your Turn Reread the last two paragraphs on page 143.

- What does Anansi do that shows how he has developed, or changed? How does this change contribute to the plot?

_____

_____

_____

_____

_____

_____

_____

Quick Tip

Writers often use dialogue to help readers learn more about how characters feel and the changes they go through.

How a character responds to what another character says can affect what happens in the story's plot. For example, what the owl says makes Anansi angry, and he behaves badly toward the birds.

Readers to Writers

When writing your own story, be clear about what causes the characters to change, how they change, and how those changes contribute to the plot, or what happens. Use what characters think, say, or do to show their development.

COLLABORATE

? **What do the selections you read and the photograph of the seahorse help you understand about animal adaptations?**

Talk About It Use the photograph and caption to talk about the leafy dragon seahorse. Discuss how the photograph shows how the seahorse survives.

Cite Text Evidence With a pencil, **trace** around the outside of the leafy dragon seahorse in the photograph. Reread the caption and **underline** what helps the animal protect itself from its predators.

Write The selections I read and this photograph help me understand

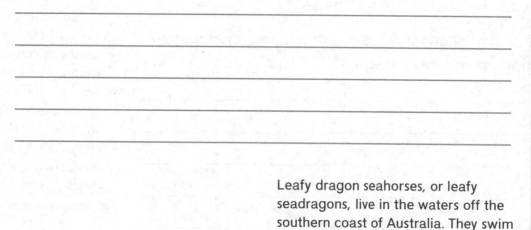

Kris Wiktor/Alamy Stock Photo

Leafy dragon seahorses, or leafy seadragons, live in the waters off the southern coast of Australia. They swim among the boulders and sea grasses in the reefs. These animals blend in with their environment to keep safe.

Quick Tip

Think about the animals you learned about and their adaptations. What are some ways animals have adapted to their environments? How are some adaptations of different animals alike?

CHECK IN 1 2 3 4

Plan a Video about Animal Adaptations

Think about what you learned about how adaptations help animals survive. What adaptations did you find the most interesting? Why? Plan a short video that shares your ideas.

1. Look at your Build Knowledge notes in your reader's notebook.

2. Choose three adaptations that interest you the most. Write a plan for a short video telling about those adaptations, why you chose them, and examples of what the audience might see and hear about the adaptations.

3. Use evidence and new vocabulary words from the texts you read to write your plan.

Think about what you learned in this text set. Fill in the bars on page 125.

Essential Question

How do animal characters change familiar stories?

Build Vocabulary

Write new words you learned about how animal characters change familiar stories. Draw lines and circles for the words you write.

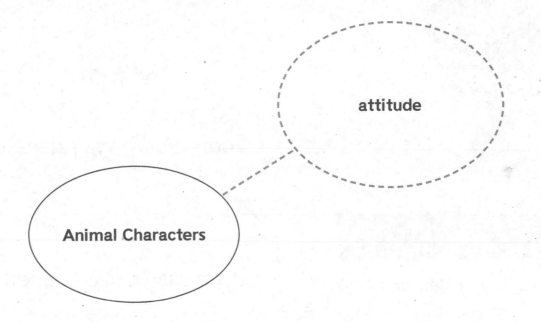

attitude

Animal Characters

Go online to **my.mheducation.com** and read the "Cast of Animals" Blast. Think about animal characters you know from the stories you have read. Then blast back your response.

Think about what you already know. Fill in the bars. There are no wrong answers here.

What I Know Now

I can read and understand a drama.

| 1 | 2 | 3 | 4 |

Key

1 = I do not understand.

2 = I understand but need more practice.

3 = I understand.

4 = I understand and can teach someone.

I can use text evidence to respond to a drama.

| 1 | 2 | 3 | 4 |

I know how animal characters change familiar stories.

| 1 | 2 | 3 | 4 |

STOP You will come back to the next page later.

Think about what you learned. Fill in the bars. What helped you the most?

What I Learned

I can read and understand a drama.

1 > 2 > 3 > 4

I can use text evidence to respond to a drama.

1 > 2 > 3 > 4

I know how animal characters change familiar stories.

1 > 2 > 3 > 4

My Goal
I can read and understand a drama.

TAKE NOTES

As you read, make note of interesting words and important details.

The Ant and the Grasshopper

Essential Question

? How do animal characters change familiar stories?

Read about how an ant teaches a grasshopper an important lesson.

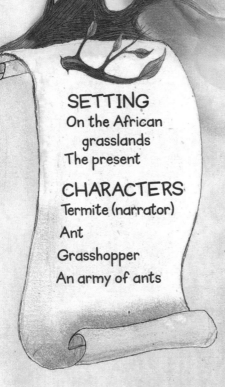

SETTING
On the African grasslands
The present

CHARACTERS
Termite (narrator)
Ant
Grasshopper
An army of ants

Scene I

(It is raining heavily on the African grasslands. Termite turns and sees the audience.)

TERMITE: *(Happily)* Yipes! I didn't see you. Welcome to the great plains of Africa! We're soggy now because it's the rainy season. Sorry. *(She shrugs and smiles.)* Today, we'll visit two very different friends of mine—Ant and Grasshopper. Maybe you have heard of them from other **familiar** stories. Let's see what my buddies are up to!

(An army of ants march in, carrying leaves filled with water. They approach Grasshopper, who lounges lazily under a plant.)

ANT: *(In a loud voice)* Company, halt! *(The ants stop.)*

GRASSHOPPER: *(Stretching and yawning)* Ant, old pal! Good to see you! I was just napping when I heard your feet pounding down the way. What's all the **commotion**?

Emily Carew Woodard

FIND TEXT EVIDENCE

Read

Termite Dialogue
Setting

Underline the sentence that tells you when this play is taking place. **Circle** the words that tell where the play is taking place. Why is knowing the setting important?

_____

_____

_____

Stage Directions
Ask and Answer Questions

Draw a box around the text evidence that describes what the ants and the grasshopper are doing. What is a question you can ask about Grasshopper?

_____

Reread

Author's Craft

Why might the author have chosen to make a play out of a fable?

SHARED READ

FIND TEXT EVIDENCE 🔍

Read

Ant Dialogue
Theme

Read all of Ant's dialogue. **Underline** the sentences that show Ant wants to teach a lesson to Grasshopper.

Ant Dialogue 4
Antonyms

Circle the antonym to the word *lazy* in the text. Based on what Ant has been saying to Grasshopper so far, which character do you think is wiser? Why?

_____

_____

Reread
Author's Craft

Compare the two scenes. What is the author's purpose for dividing the play into two scenes?

ANT: (*Looking annoyed*) Grasshopper, have you noticed what falls from the sky above you?

(*Ant stands at attention and points up at a cloud. Grasshopper sleepily rises and stands next to Ant. He looks at the sky.*)

ANT: Rain, Grasshopper! Rain falls from the sky! And when there is rain, there is work to be done.

GRASSHOPPER: (*Smiling, then scratching his head*) Huh?

ANT: (*Sighing*) You should be collecting water for a time when it is unavailable. Instead, you lie here without a care for the future.

GRASSHOPPER: (*Laughing*) Oh, don't be so serious, ol' buddy! There is plenty of water now, and that's all that matters. You need to relax! You're much too tense. Why don't you make napping your new **specialty** instead of all this silly toil? Stop working so hard all the time!

ANT: (*Shaking his head as he grows **frustrated***) The rainy season will not last forever, Grasshopper. Your carefree **attitude** will disappear with the water, and soon you will regret being lazy and wish you had been more energetic.

(*The ants march off as Grasshopper continues to laugh.*)

Scene II

selfish →

(*It is a few months later, and the plains are now dusty, dry, and brown. Grasshopper, appearing weak and sickly, knocks on Ant's door. Ant, seeming strong and healthy, opens the door.*)

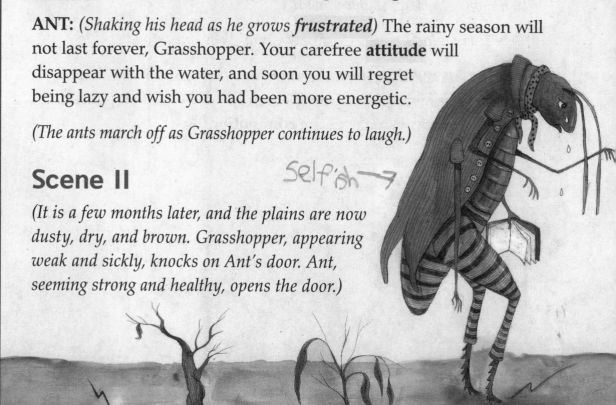

GRASSHOPPER: *(Nervously)* Hi there, pal . . . I was in the neighborhood. Boy, can you believe how hot it is? So . . . uh . . . I was wondering if maybe . . . by chance . . . you might have some water for your old friend.

(Ant tries to close the door, but Grasshopper quickly grabs it.)

GRASSHOPPER: *(Begging wildly)* PLEASE, Ant! I am so thirsty! There isn't a drop of water anywhere!

ANT: *(After a pause)* We ants worked hard to collect this water, but we cannot let you suffer. *(Giving Grasshopper a sip of water)* Do not think us **selfish**, but we can only share a few drops with you. I warned you that this time would come. If you had prepared, you would not be in this situation.

(Grasshopper walks slowly away. Termite watches him go.)

TERMITE: Although Ant has done a good deed, tired, **cranky** Grasshopper must still search for water. Grasshopper learned an important lesson today. Next time, he will follow Ant's advice!

Summarize

Use your notes to summarize what happens in "The Ant and the Grasshopper."

FIND TEXT EVIDENCE

Read

Ant Dialogue

Theme

Underline the sentence that shows the lesson Ant was trying to teach Grasshopper.

Stage Directions

Read the entire page. **Circle** a stage direction that includes Ant and Grasshopper. How do you know which character speaks next?

_____

_____

Reread

Author's Craft

What is the author's purpose for including Termite in the play?

Vocabulary

Use the example sentences to talk with a partner about each word. Then answer the questions.

annoyed

I was **annoyed** when my cats woke me up very early in the morning.

What is a synonym for *annoyed*?

_____

attitude

The girls had a good **attitude** when asked to volunteer for the book drive.

Describe your attitude about doing chores.

_____

_____

commotion

The ducks made a **commotion** with their quacking and splashing.

What is an example of something that can make a commotion?

_____

_____

cranky

Neil feels **cranky** when he is hungry.

What makes you feel cranky?

_____

familiar

I did not get lost because I took a **familiar** route from the bus stop to my house.

What is a familiar sound on the playground?

_____

 Build Your Word List Reread Termite's dialogue on page 153. Circle the word *soggy*. In your reader's notebook, use a word web to write antonyms for the word. For example, one antonym is *dry*. Use a thesaurus to look up other antonyms.

frustrated

The student was **frustrated** by the difficult assignment.

What makes you feel frustrated?

_____

_____

selfish

The two pals are not **selfish,** and they share everything.

How would you describe a selfish person?

_____

_____

specialty

My uncle is a good cook and his **specialty** is spaghetti.

If you were a cook, what would be your specialty?

_____

_____

Antonyms

As you read "The Ant and the Grasshopper," you may come across a word you don't know. Sometimes the author will use an antonym, a word or phrase that means the opposite of another word or phrase you might see in a nearby sentence.

🔍 FIND TEXT EVIDENCE

On page 154, I'm not sure what the word carefree means. I can use the word serious to help me figure out what carefree means.

"Oh, don't be so serious, ol' buddy! There is plenty of water now, and that's all that matters. You need to relax!"

Your Turn Write an antonym for each word below in "The Ant and the Grasshopper." Write the meaning for each antonym.

halt, page 153 _____

tense, page 154 _____

sickly, page 154_____

_____

CHECK IN 1 2 3 4

Ask and Answer Questions

When you read a selection, you may not understand all of it. It helps to stop and ask yourself questions. As you read "The Ant and the Grasshopper," ask questions about what you don't understand. Then read to find the answers.

 FIND TEXT EVIDENCE

After reading Scene I, you may ask yourself what happens in Africa after the rainy season ends. Reread Scene II of "The Ant and the Grasshopper" to find the answer.

Page 154

Scene II
(It is a few months later, and the plains are now dusty, dry, and brown. Grasshopper, appearing weak and sickly, knocks on Ant's door. Ant, seeming strong and healthy, opens the door.)

I read that the land is "dusty, dry, and brown." Grasshopper is weak. This makes me understand that there are long periods of time when no rain falls in Africa.

> **Quick Tip**
>
> As you read, write down questions you have on sticky notes or a piece of paper. Then look for the answer as you continue to read. If you didn't find the answers, try going back and rereading scenes to see if you missed some information.

 Your Turn Reread the last paragraph on page 155. Ask and answer a question about this paragraph.

_____

_____

_____

CHECK IN 1 2 3 4

Elements of a Play

"The Ant and the Grasshopper" is a play, or drama. Plays include characters' dialogue, setting information, and stage directions. Some plays are separated into different scenes, or parts. Like other narratives, a play has a plot. The setting in a play can be very important to the plot, or what happens.

FIND TEXT EVIDENCE

I can tell that "The Ant and the Grasshopper" is a play. The author describes the setting. There is also dialogue, the lines that actors speak. The characters' names appear in capital letters before the lines they speak. The stage directions tell the actors what to do.

Page 153

Scene I

(It is raining heavily on the African grasslands. Termite turns and sees the audience.)

SETTING
On the African grasslands
The present

CHARACTERS
Termite (narrator)
Ant
Grasshopper
An army of ants

TERMITE: *(Happily)* Yipes! I didn't see you. Welcome to the great plains of Africa! We're soggy now because it's the rainy season. Sorry. *(She shrugs and smiles.)* Today, we'll visit two very different friends of mine—Ant and Grasshopper. Maybe you have heard of them from other **familiar** stories. Let's see what my buddies are up to!

(An army of ants march in, carrying leaves filled with water. They approach Grasshopper, who lounges lazily under a plant.)

ANT: *(In a loud voice)* Company, halt! *(The ants stop.)*

GRASSHOPPER: *(Stretching and yawning)* Ant, old pal! Good to see you! I was just napping when I heard your feet pounding down the way. What's all the **commotion**?

The setting, character development, events, and conflict all contribute to the play's, or drama's, plot. Think how you can use these elements to develop your plot in your own writing. For example, how can setting affect your plot? Remember, setting includes the weather.

Scene
Tells when a new scene begins.

Setting
Describes where and when the play takes place.

Stage Directions
Tells the actors how to speak their dialogue and how to move.

Your Turn Discuss the two scenes in "The Ant and the Grasshopper." How does the change in setting contribute to the plot, or what happens?

_____

_____

_____

_____

CHECK IN 1 2 3 4

Theme

The theme of a story is the message or big idea about life that the author wants to tell. Themes can be implied or stated. To identify the theme and how it develops, pay attention to how the characters respond to situations and what they learn. What deeper ideas do the details suggest?

🔍 FIND TEXT EVIDENCE

As I reread "The Ant and the Grasshopper," the different actions of Ant and Grasshopper in the rainy season seem like important clues to the development of the theme. So do Ant's words about collecting water.

Look for details that help you identify the theme.

Clue
Ant collects water during the rainy season. Grasshopper naps.

Clue
Ant tells Grasshopper he should collect water.

Theme
Hard work pays off

Your Turn Reread "The Ant and the Grasshopper." What other details give clues about the theme and show its development? Add them to the graphic organizer on page 161. Use the clues to figure out the theme. Explain your ideas to your partner.

CHECK IN 1 > 2 > 3 > 4

Ant made sure he had **Clue** what he needed for the harsh weathes.

↓

Grass hopper laughs and **Clue** tells A

↓

Grasshopper comes to **Clue** Ant begging for water

↓

Theme

My Goal I can use text evidence to respond to a drama.

Respond to Reading

Discuss the prompt below. Use your notes and text evidence to support your response.

What is your opinion of Ant and his actions in this story? Why do you feel that way?

_____

_____

_____

_____

_____

_____

_____

_____

_____

_____

_____

_____

_____

Quick Tip

Review the story by summarizing the plot and theme. Then use these sentence starters to discuss the text.

- *I agree/don't agree with Ant's actions because . . .*
- *I think that Grasshopper . . .*
- *I think that Ant . . .*

Grammar Connections

Check your use of singular and plural nouns.

When a singular noun ends with a consonant followed by the letter *y,* change the *y* to *i* and add *-es.* For example, *story* becomes *stories.*

When a singular noun ends with *s, ss, sh, ch, x,* or *s,* add *-es.*

CHECK IN 1 2 3 4

SCIENCE

Make a Food Web

Make a food web that shows how plants and animals in a pond ecosystem get energy, or food. Follow the research process to create the food web and write a short report. Work with a partner.

COLLABORATE

Step 1 **Set a Goal** Generate questions that you want your research to answer about plants and animals that live in a pond and the food they eat.

Step 2 **Identify Sources** Use books, magazines, and websites to find information about a pond's ecosystem.

Step 3 **Find and Record Information**
Ponds in different parts of the country have different ecosystems. As you research and learn about ponds, choose a pond ecosystem to focus on. Decide what plants and animals you will include in your web. Take notes, find images, and cite your sources.

Step 4 **Organize and Synthesize Information** Plan out your food web. Include the Sun in your web. Choose or create images. Decide what information to include in your report.

Step 5 **Create and Present** Create a final food web and report. Decide how you will present the information to the class.

Forest Food Web

The plants and trees in the food web above get their energy from the Sun. What is another connection shown in this web?

_____

_____

_____

CHECK IN ⟩ 1 ⟩ 2 ⟩ 3 ⟩ 4

Ranita, The Frog Princess

 How does the author help you understand what the Spanish words mean?

Literature Anthology: pages 110–125

 Talk About It Reread the dialogue on **Literature Anthology** page 114. Turn to your partner and talk about what helps you to understand the Spanish words in italics.

Cite Text Evidence What clues help you figure out each word's meaning? Record the words and clues here.

Word	Text Evidence

Evaluate Information

The author tells you in the beginning of the play that the action takes place in Mexico. Review the characters' names and the Spanish words that appear throughout the play. How does the use of Spanish words and names in the play help give you a better sense of the setting?

Write I know what the Spanish words mean because the author _____

_____

_____

CHECK IN 1 2 3 4

How do you know how the other characters feel about Felipe?

 Talk About It Reread page 116 of the **Literature Anthology**. Turn to your partner and talk about how the author shows what the other characters in the play are feeling.

Cite Text Evidence Which words describe how the characters feel about Felipe? Use text evidence to explain how you know.

Character $\longrightarrow$	Text Evidence
$\longrightarrow$	
$\longrightarrow$	
$\longrightarrow$	
$\longrightarrow$	

Write I know how the other characters feel about Felipe because the author _____

_____

_____

_____

CHECK IN ⟩ 1 ⟩ 2 ⟩ 3 ⟩ 4 ⟩

? **How does the setting contribute to the plot of the play?**

COLLABORATE

Talk About It Reread **Literature Anthology** page 112. Turn to your partner and talk about where the characters are and what they are doing.

Cite Text Evidence What conclusion can you make about the society in which the characters live? Write the text evidence in the chart.

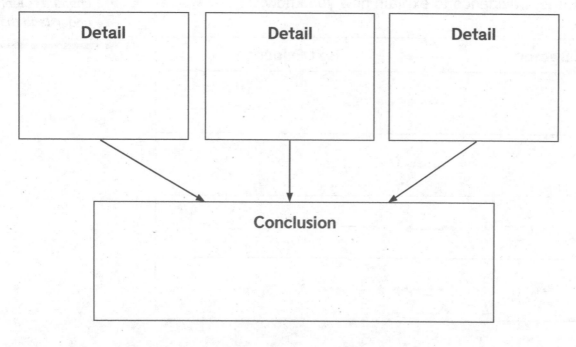

| Detail | Detail | Detail |

Conclusion

Write The setting is important to the plot because_____

_____

_____

_____

_____

Quick Tip

Setting includes the type of society, or community, where a story takes place. To better understand a setting, think about the type of society in the story and how people in the society behave.

 Make Inferences

Think about the things Man One, Man Two, and Man Three say to each other and the way Felipe responds to them. What inference can you make about the way life was in Mexico at the time the play takes place? How is Felipe's life different from the men's?

CHECK IN 1 2 3 4

Respond to Reading

Discuss the prompt below. Use your notes and text evidence to support your response.

Which character changes the most? Why is this change important to the story?

_____

_____

_____

_____

_____

_____

_____

_____

_____

_____

_____

_____

_____

Quick Tip

Use these sentence starters to organize your text evidence.

- *I think [character's name] changes the most . . .*
- *In the beginning, . . .*
- *By the end, . . .*

CHECK IN 1 > 2 > 3 > 4

Pecos Bill and the Bear Lake Monster

Literature Anthology:
pages 128–131

1   Have you ever heard tell of Pecos Bill? The cowboy raised by coyotes for seventeen years? The one who lassoed a tornado out of the sky using a live rattlesnake as a lariat? And dug the Rio Grande because his cattle felt thirsty and needed water?...

2   Pecos Bill was spending some time riding the range and herding cattle with a bunch of cowpokes. Late one night around a campfire, a cowpoke from Utah started telling stories about the Bear Lake monster. He said the monster looked like a snake with tiny legs and was over 100 miles long. One of the monster's favorite tricks was to suddenly appear in front of swimmers just to hear them shriek. Of course, it also ate a couple of those swimmers for lunch. Then there was the time a herd of pronghorn antelope went to drink from the lake. The snake slurped the whole herd down like it was nothing more than a big gulp of sweet tea. Another time, the monster had an itch on its tail. It got so frustrated trying to scratch that itch, the waves from the lake flooded the shore for days.

Reread paragraph 1. **Draw a box** around three things that show you that Pecos Bill is a larger-than-life character. Write them here.

_____

_____

_____

_____

COLLABORATE

Discuss how the author uses descriptive language to describe the Bear Lake monster. What do the characters have in common?

_____

_____

_____

_____

_____

1   When Bill got to Bear Lake he was mighty hot and thirsty. He waded right into the cool, clear water and swam out a mile or two. All of a sudden, the water churned and foamed and ten-foot waves started crashing over Bill's head. A monster reared out of the water with its mouth open and roared. Bill had seen caverns smaller than that snake's mouth. Its roar shook the surrounding mountains. Without missing a beat, Pecos Bill jumped onto the monster's neck and slipped a loop of rope into its mouth. Then he held the ends like reins.

2   To say the snake was as cranky as a grizzly that's been stung by a swarm of hornets is understating the matter. The monster twisted and turned its scaly back trying to buck Bill off. But Bill didn't budge. The winds shrieked and howled around Bill, whipping up the waves to higher and higher peaks. So much water got splashed around that the whole lake turned into a giant waterspout!

Reread paragraph 2. **Circle** what happened to Pecos Bill when the monster tried to buck him off. **Underline** the descriptive language the author uses to help you picture what happens next.

COLLABORATE

Look at the illustration below and read the caption. Discuss how the snake changes from the beginning of the story to the end. Write the text evidence here.

_____

_____

The monster snake from Bear Lake, Utah, still lives in the loch to this day. Only now it's so shy and frightened that only a few people have ever seen it.

? How does the author use the comparison of Pecos Bill to the Bear Lake monster to create suspense?

Talk About It Reread both excerpts on pages 168–169. Talk with a partner about the descriptions of Pecos Bill and the Bear Lake monster.

Cite Text Evidence How does describing the characters' past actions on page 168 build suspense for the battle on page 169? Write text evidence here and explain how the descriptions build suspense.

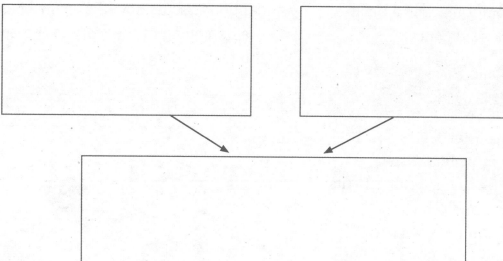

Write Why does the author begin the tale by describing both Pecos Bill's and the monster's past actions?

_____

_____

_____

CHECK IN 1 2 3 4

Hyperbole

An exaggeration makes something sound bigger or better than it really is. For example, you are exaggerating if you say, "I'm so hungry I can eat a horse." Writers exaggerate to add drama to a story and make characters larger than life. Those exaggerations are called hyperbole. Exaggerations are often used in tall tales like the one you just read about Pecos Bill.

FIND TEXT EVIDENCE

In paragraph 2 on page 168 of "Pecos Bill and the Bear Lake Monster," the author uses hyperbole to tell what happens after the monster scratches an itch. The author tells us that the waves from the lake flooded the shore for days. We can tell that the author is exaggerating to make the monster an incredible, larger-than-life character.

> Another time, the monster had an itch on its tail. It got so frustrated trying to scratch that itch, the waves from the lake flooded the shore for days.

Your Turn Reread paragraph 2 on page 169.

- What words does the author use to describe what happened when Pecos Bill and the monster wrestled? _____

_____

- How does hyperbole help you picture the battle?

_____

How are the *Ranita, The Frog Princess,* "Pecos Bill and the Bear Lake Monster," and the illustration on this page similar?

Talk About It Look at the illustration. What are the animals doing? How do you think they feel? Why might the artist have chosen animals as the characters instead of people?

Cite Text Evidence **Circle** the images that help you understand how the animals in the illustration feel. **Draw a box** around the things the animals are doing that people do.

Write The selections I read and the illustration all

_____

_____

_____

_____

_____

_____

_____

_____

_____

_____

CHECK IN ⟩ 1 ⟩ 2 ⟩ 3 ⟩ 4 ⟩

My Goal I know how animal characters change familiar stories.

Write a Story

The stories you read all have animal characters in them. What do the animal characters have in common? What else do the stories have in common?

1 Look at your Build Knowledge notes in your reader's notebook.

2 Make a list of three things the stories have in common. The first thing on your list can be that the stories all have animal characters. Write two more ideas for your list. Use evidence from the texts to come up with your ideas.

3 Use your list to write a quick short story. Your story should use all three ideas from your list. Try to include new vocabulary.

Think about what you learned in this text set. Fill in the bars on page 151.

Build Knowledge

Build Vocabulary

Write new words you learned about how animals inspire writers.
Draw lines and circles for the words you write.

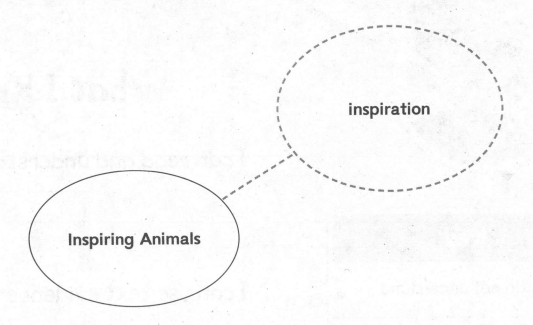

inspiration

Inspiring Animals

Go online to **my.mheducation.com** and read the "Inspiring Animals" Blast.
Think about your favorite story about an animal. How are writers inspired by
animals? Then blast back your response.

Think about what you already know. Fill in the bars. You'll keep learning more.

What I Know Now

I can read and understand poetry.

| 1 | 2 | 3 | 4 |

I can use text evidence to respond to poetry.

| 1 | 2 | 3 | 4 |

I know how animals inspire writers.

| 1 | 2 | 3 | 4 |

Key

1 =	I do not understand.
2 =	I understand but need more practice.
3 =	I understand.
4 =	I understand and can teach someone.

STOP You will come back to the next page later.

Think about what you learned. Fill in the bars. Keep up the good work!

What I Learned

I can read and understand poetry.

1 2 3 4

I can use text evidence to respond to poetry.

1 2 3 4

I know how animals inspire writers.

1 2 3 4

My Goal
I can read and understand poetry.

TAKE NOTES

As you read, make note of interesting words and important details.

_____

_____

_____

_____

_____

_____

_____

_____

_____

_____

_____

_____

_____

_____

DOG

A brown boomerang,
my dog flies off, arcs his way
back into my arms.

— Jeffrey Boyle

Essential Question

? **How are writers inspired by animals?**

Read how poets use creative thinking to write about animals.

THE EAGLE

He clasps the crag with crooked hands;
Close to the sun in lonely lands,
Ring'd with the azure world, he stands.

The wrinkled sea beneath him crawls;
He watches from his mountain walls,
And like a thunderbolt he falls.

— Alfred, Lord Tennyson

Emily Carew Woodard

FIND TEXT EVIDENCE

Read

Page 178

Character Perspective

Underline words that let you know the relationship between the dog and the speaker. What is that relationship? How do you think the speaker feels about the dog? Why?

The speaker is the dog's owner. I think he loves his dog.

Page 179

Similes and Metaphors

Draw a box around what the speaker is comparing the eagle's claws to.

Reread

Author's Craft

What language hints at how the speaker feels about the eagle? Use text evidence.

SHARED READ

FIND TEXT EVIDENCE 🔍

Read

Page 180

Character Perspective

Underline pronouns that tell whose perspective, or thoughts and feelings, the poet is writing about. Who is the poet writing about?

Rhyme and Structure

Circle the rhyming words in the first two stanzas. What do you notice about the location of the rhyming words?

The rhyming words are at the end of the 2nd and 4th lines

Read the second stanza aloud. Does the second stanza have a consistent rhythm, or meter?

Reread

Author's Craft

How would the poem be different if the speaker was not a character in the poem?

180 Unit 2 • Text Set 3

CHIMPANZEE

From branch to branch on outstretched arms,
From tree to ground I leap.
When I want to eat a snack,
I stick a stick in a termite heap.

I use my teeth to rip off leaves
And make the branch all bare,
Then find the hole the bugs come out
And patiently wait there.

My skinny branch becomes a bridge,
As brittle bugs climb up the stick.
I pick them off one by one
And crunch them like potato chips!

— Ellen Lee

cute Rat

Rat

Teeth like jackhammers,
I chew through concrete for fun,
bring the outdoors in!

— Rosa Sandoval

Make Connections

What animal would you write a poem about? What details about the animal would you focus on?

FIND TEXT EVIDENCE

Read

Page 181

Character Perspective

Underline the details that tell how the rat feels about its actions.

Similes and Metaphors

Circle the word that tells you two things are being compared. Write the two things being compared.

_____

Haiku

How many syllables are in the first and last lines? Write the answer.

_____

Reread

Author's Craft

Reread "Chimpanzee" and "Rat." Compare and contrast the two poems.

Vocabulary

Use the example sentences to talk with a partner about each word. Then answer the questions.

brittle

The dry, **brittle** leaf fell apart when I closed my hand around it.

What is something else that is brittle?

Thin lager of ice,
_____

creative

Our team was **creative** and built robots for the competition.

Describe a time when you were creative.

_____

_____

descriptive

The zookeeper gave a **descriptive** talk about giraffes, telling what they look and act like.

Use descriptive language to discuss your favorite activity.

_____

_____

outstretched

Three seagulls glided through the air on **outstretched** wings.

What is an antonym for the word *outstretched*?

_____

_____

Poetry Terms

metaphor

"The huge garbage truck is a monster" is a **metaphor** because it compares two unlike things without using *like* or *as*.

Give another example of a metaphor.

_____

_____

simile

"The long grass is like hair" is a **simile** because it compares two unlike things using *like* or *as*.

Give another example of a simile.

_____

_____

rhyme

Two words **rhyme** when they end with the same sound, such as *claw* and *draw*.

What word rhymes with *fall*?

_____

_____

meter

Meter is the pattern of stressed and unstressed syllables in a poem.

How does a strong meter affect the rhythm of a poem?

_____

_____

Build Your Word List Reread "The Eagle" on page 179. Underline two interesting words. In your reader's notebook, write the two words. Use an online or print thesaurus to find two synonyms for each word. Write the synonyms next to each word.

Similes and Metaphors

Two types of figurative language are similes and metaphors. A simile compares two things using the words *like* or *as*—for example, *straight as an arrow*. A metaphor compares two things without the words *like* or *as*—for example, *the grass was a green carpet*.

🔍 FIND TEXT EVIDENCE

When I read "Chimpanzee" on page 180, I see that the poet uses a simile in the last stanza to describe how the chimpanzee is eating the termites.

I pick them off one by one
And crunch them like potato chips!

Your Turn Reread the first stanza of "The Eagle" on page 179 and identify the metaphor. In your reader's notebook, rewrite the metaphor as a simile.

_____

_____

CHECK IN 1 2 3 4

Alessandra Cimatoribus

Rhyme and Structure

Words **rhyme** when their endings sound the same. **Structure** includes the arrangement of sounds, words, lines, and stanzas in a poem. **Meter** is a type of sound structure. Meter is the arrangement of stressed, or emphasized, and unstressed syllables. This arrangement creates a rhythm, or pattern of sound.

 FIND TEXT EVIDENCE

Reread the first stanza in "The Eagle" on page 179 aloud. Listen for the end rhymes and to the rhythm of the meter.

> He clasps the crag with crooked hands;
> Close to the sun in lonely lands,
> Ring'd with the azure world, he stands.
>
> The wrinkled sea beneath him crawls;
> He watches from his mountain walls,
> And like a thunderbolt he falls.

Rhyme *One way the end rhymes add meaning to the poem is by drawing attention to how the speaker is describing the eagle's action and the location.*

Meter *Read the second stanza aloud. A stressed syllable follows each unstressed syllable, which creates a regular rhythm. This makes each line feel equally important.*

 Your Turn Reread the second stanza of "The Eagle." What words rhyme? What idea do you think the speaker is trying to communicate?

_____

_____

_____

_____

Quick Tip

A poem's rhyme pattern and other structures, such as meter, draw attention to certain words, images, and feelings. Rhyme and structure can also emphasize connections between certain words, images, and feelings. All of this helps to create meaning and express the ideas of a poem.

CHECK IN 1 2 3 4

Lyric Poetry and Haiku

Lyric poetry expresses personal thoughts and feelings. Lyric poetry has a musical quality, or sound. It often has end rhymes and a consistent, or regular, meter.

Haiku uses three short lines to describe a scene or a moment. It has a first and last line of five syllables and a second line of seven syllables.

 FIND TEXT EVIDENCE

"The Eagle" is a lyric poem because it tells how the speaker feels about the eagle. It also has end rhymes and a consistent meter.

Page 179

THE EAGLE

He clasps the crag with crooked hands;
Close to the sun in lonely lands,
Ring'd with the azure world, he stands.

The wrinkled sea beneath him crawls;
He watches from his mountain walls,
And like a thunderbolt he falls.

— Alfred, Lord Tennyson

The speaker describes the eagle as "close to the sun in lonely lands." This tells me that the speaker sees the eagle as uniquely powerful.

 Your Turn Reread the poem "Dog" on page 178. Identify the form of the poem and give evidence. Then tell what is being described.

_____

_____

_____

_____

CHECK IN 1 2 3 4

Character Perspective

Character perspective refers to the attitude of the characters, or the way they view, think, or feel about something. Paying attention to how characters describe events will help you to understand their perspective on the event.

FIND TEXT EVIDENCE

In "Chimpanzee," the chimpanzee describes how it gets food. I will reread the first stanza on page 180 and find the details that give me clues to the chimpanzee's perspective on getting food.

Details
From tree to ground I leap
When I want to eat a snack, / I stick a stick in a termite heap.

↓

Character Perspective
The chimpanzee knows where to find food.

Your Turn Reread the rest of "Chimpanzee" on page 180. List important details in the graphic organizer on page 187. Use the details to figure out the chimpanzee's perspective.

Quick Tip

In some poems, the speaker, or the voice telling the poem, is also a character in the poem. The pronouns *I, me,* and *my* show that the speaker is also the character and is telling about his or her own perspective, or feelings.

CHECK IN   1   2   3   4

Details

Character Perspective

COLLABORATE

Respond to Reading

Discuss the prompt below. Use your notes and text evidence to support your response.

How do you feel about each animal after reading the poems? Explain your answer.

_____

_____

_____

_____

_____

_____

_____

_____

_____

_____

_____

_____

Quick Tip

Use these sentence starters to discuss the poems and organize your ideas.

• *After reading . . .*

• *The speaker says . . .*

• *. . . made me think about . . .*

Readers to Writers

When you write about a poem, remember that the poet is the writer of the poem. The speaker is the narrator, or voice, telling the poem.

CHECK IN 〉1〉2〉3〉4〉

Present Fun Animal Facts

COLLABORATE

Animals can inspire all kinds of creative projects. Choose an animal in your state. Follow the research process to find five fun, unusual facts about the animal. Use the facts to create a project, such as a graphic comic, a poem, a collage, or a digital poster. Work with a partner.

Step 1 **Set a Goal** Brainstorm animals in your state. Choose an animal. Then decide which type of project to do.

Step 2 **Identify Sources** What are some sources you can use to research your animal?

_____

_____

Step 3 **Find and Record Information** Find fun facts about your animal and take notes. Include one or more inherited behaviors. Look for any visuals that you want to use. Keep track of your sources so that you can correctly cite them in a bibliography.

Step 4 **Organize and Synthesize Information** Decide how best to use your information for your project.

Step 5 **Create and Present** Create your project. Make a bibliography listing the sources you used. After you finish, you will share your project and bibliography with the class.

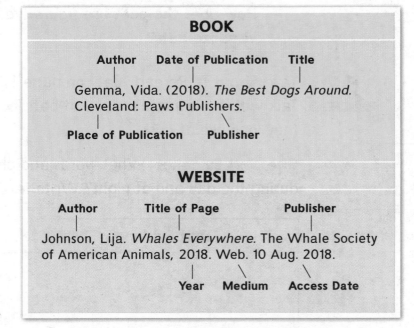

BOOK

Author   Date of Publication   Title
| | |
Gemma, Vida. (2018). *The Best Dogs Around.*
Cleveland: Paws Publishers.
| |
Place of Publication   **Publisher**

WEBSITE

Author   Title of Page   Publisher
| | |
Johnson, Lija. *Whales Everywhere.* The Whale Society of American Animals, 2018. Web. 10 Aug. 2018.
| | |
Year   **Medium**   **Access Date**

Bibliographies include information about a source. In the list, the information is presented in a certain order, usually alphabetical.

CHECK IN ⟩ 1 ⟩ 2 ⟩ 3 ⟩ 4 ⟩

Poetry

Literature Anthology: pages 132–134

? **How does the poet use figurative language to help you visualize bats?**

Talk About It Reread "Bat" on page 133 of the **Literature Anthology**. Talk with a partner about what bats look like during the day and what they look like at dusk.

Cite Text Evidence What words and phrases help you picture the bats during the day and at night? Write text evidence in the chart.

Text Evidence	What I Visualize

Write The poet helps me visualize bats by _____

_____

_____

 Make Inferences

Identify the similes in the first stanza. Then identify the imagery in the second stanza. Use this information to make an inference about how the speaker feels about bats.

CHECK IN 1 2 3 4

? How does each poet use words and phrases to create a different mood?

Talk About It With a partner, reread "The Grasshopper Springs" and "Fireflies at Dusk" on page 134 of the **Literature Anthology.** Talk about how each poem makes you feel.

Cite Text Evidence What words help to create a certain mood in the poems? Write and explain text evidence in the chart.

Poem	Text Evidence	Why Is This Effective?
"The Grasshopper Springs"		
"Fireflies at Dusk"		

Write The poets create a mood in their poem by _____

_____

CHECK IN 1 2 3 4

Respond to Reading

COLLABORATE Discuss the prompt below. Use your notes and evidence from the text to support your answer.

What can you learn about the speakers in the poems from how they describe the animals?

_____

_____

_____

_____

_____

_____

_____

_____

_____

_____

_____

_____

_____

_____

Quick Tip

Use these sentence starters to talk about and cite evidence in the text.

- _In . . . the speaker says . . ._
- _This shows that . . ._
- _I think that the speaker . . ._

CHECK IN 1 2 3 4

Fog

 How does the poet use words and phrases to help you visualize how fog is like a cat?

Literature Anthology: pages 136-137

 Talk About It Read "Fog" on page 136 of the **Literature Anthology** aloud to a partner. Talk about how the poet describes what fog is like.

Cite Text Evidence What words and phrases help you picture how fog is like a cat? Write text evidence in the chart.

Quick Tip

When poets compare two unlike things, they are creating a simile or metaphor. This figurative language helps the reader visualize what the poet is describing. It also lends artistry to the poem.

Text Evidence	What I Visualize

Write The poet helps me visualize how fog is like a cat by _____

_____

_____

_____

CHECK IN 1 2 3 4

White Cat Winter

? **How do the poets use words and phrases to create mood?**

Talk About It Reread the poems on pages 136 and 137 of the **Literature Anthology**. Talk with a partner about how each poem makes you feel.

Cite Text Evidence What words and phrases help create a mood in each poem? Write text evidence and describe the mood.

Quick Tip

Remember that mood is the feeling a poem or story gives the reader. How do you feel when you read these poems? Happy, excited, sad, calm, afraid? What words give you that feeling? Why do they make you feel this way?

Text Evidence	Mood

Write The poets create mood by _____

_____

_____

CHECK IN 1 2 3 4

Imagery and Assonance

Readers to Writers

When you write a poem, think about what poetry elements you can use to help create the mood of the poem.

- Imagery uses sensory language, or words that appeal to the senses, to show what things look, sound, feel, taste, or smell like.
- Assonance, like meter and rhyme patterns, is a type of sound structure that helps connect ideas and add meaning to the poem.

Different poetry elements can contribute to the mood of a poem and add to meaning. Two of these elements are **imagery** and **assonance**. Imagery is the use of specific language to create pictures in a reader's mind. Assonance is the repetition of vowel sounds in two or more words, such as *row* and *bone*. Assonance can be used to emphasize or connect ideas.

FIND TEXT EVIDENCE

In "White Cat Winter," on page 137 of the **Literature Anthology**, the long *e* sound is repeated in *creeps, asleep,* and *beside.* This use of assonance emphasizes a quiet mood by calling attention to the imagery of creeping "along low walls of stone" and falling "asleep / beside the barn."

Your Turn Read the poem "White Cat Winter" again.

- What other examples of assonance are in the poem? _____

_____

_____

- What words create imagery that help you visualize the farm? How do these images affect the mood of the poem?

_____

_____

_____

CHECK IN 1 2 3 4

? How does Lewis Carroll use the crocodile as inspiration for his poem? How is Carroll's poem similar to the other animal poems you read this week?

Talk About It Read "How Doth the Little Crocodile." Talk with a partner about how Lewis Carroll describes the crocodile.

Cite Text Evidence **Circle** words and phrases in the poem that help you visualize the crocodile.

Write The poems I read this week help me understand how writers are inspired by animals. The way Lewis Carroll is inspired by the crocodile is similar to _____

_____

_____

_____

_____

_____

_____

How Doth the Little Crocodile

How doth the little crocodile
Improve his shining tail,
And pour the waters of the Nile
On every golden scale!

How cheerfully he seems to grin,
How neatly spreads his claws,
And welcomes little fishes in
With gently smiling jaws!

— Lewis Carroll

CHECK IN 1 2 3 4

My Goal: I know how writers are inspired by animals.

Write a Poem

Think about what you learned about how writers are inspired by animals. What do the different poets want the readers to know about animals?

1. Look at your Build Knowledge notes in your reader's notebook.

2. Think about how the animals in the poems are described. What does that tell you about what might have inspired the poets to write the poems? Jot down your ideas.

3. Use your ideas to write a poem that gives reasons why poets might be inspired to write about animals. Include examples from the poems you read. Try to include new vocabulary words.

Think about what you learned in this text set. Fill in the bars on page 177.

Think about what you already know. Then fill in the bars. Meeting your goals may take time.

What I Know Now

I can write an expository essay.

I can synthesize information from three sources.

Key	
1 =	I do not understand.
2 =	I understand but need more practice.
3 =	I understand.
4 =	I understand and can teach someone.

Think about what you learned.
Fill in the bars. What do you want to work on more?

What I Learned

I can write an expository essay.

1   2   3   4

I can synthesize information from three sources.

1   2   3   4

WRITE TO SOURCES

You will answer an expository writing prompt using sources and a rubric.

ANALYZE THE RUBRIC

A rubric tells you what needs to be included in your writing.

Purpose, Focus, and Organization

Read the second bullet. Why is it important?

_____

_____

_____

Evidence and Elaboration

Read the third bullet. What is the connection between elaborative techniques and the central idea?

_____

_____

_____

Evidence and Elaboration

Underline examples of elaboration in the third bullet.

Expository Writing Rubric

Purpose, Focus, and Organization • Score 4

- stays focused on the purpose, audience, and task
- **clearly presents and fully develops the central idea about a topic**
- uses transitional strategies, such as words and phrases, to connect ideas
- uses a logical text structure to organize information
- begins with a strong introduction and ends with a strong conclusion

Evidence and Elaboration • Score 4

- effectively supports the central idea with convincing facts and details
- has strong examples of relevant evidence, or supporting details, from multiple sources
- uses elaborative techniques, such as facts, examples, definitions, and quotations from sources
- expresses interesting ideas clearly using precise language
- uses appropriate academic and domain-specific language
- uses different sentence structures

Turn to page 240 for the complete Expository Writing Rubric.

Central Idea

Presenting the Central Idea A strong expository essay presents a clear central idea. Read the paragraph below. The central idea is highlighted.

> In November of 2019, a scientific study came out. It told about mercury levels in the Great Lakes' big game fish. The study was not good news. It hit close to home because I love fishing in the Great Lakes. It showed that zebra mussels are destroying the food chain. They eat plants that were part of the diet of large fish like the lake trout. As a result, the lake trout must now eat large quantities of small fish that are high in mercury. Zebra mussels are an example of an invasive species, a species that is not native to the Great Lakes. **Invasive species can harm the environment. They can also disrupt human activities, such as safely eating local fish.**

Audience

Writers have an audience in mind when they write. They make choices about what to include based on their audience. For example, if a scientist wrote an article for a children's magazine, what might she include to help kids understand the terms she used?

What does the central idea tell you about the focus of the essay?

_____

_____

_____

_____

Details Writers use relevant details to support and develop the central idea. These relevant, or supporting, details help keep the essay focused on the central idea. Strong writers do not include unimportant details in their writing.

Read the paragraph above. Cross out an unimportant detail that does NOT support the central idea.

ANALYZE THE STUDENT MODEL

Paragraph 1

Write a detail from Sonya's introduction that caught your attention.

_____

_____

_____

Reread the first paragraph of Sonya's essay. The central idea is highlighted.

Paragraph 2

What is an example of relevant evidence that Sonya uses to support her central idea?

_____

_____

_____

Circle the details that tell you a result of the invasive species.

Student Model: Expository Essay

Sonya responded to the Writing Prompt: _Write an expository essay to present to your class about why invasive species are a problem near the Great Lakes._ Read Sonya's essay below.

1   In November of 2019, a scientific study came out. It told about mercury levels in the Great Lakes' big game fish. The study was not good news. It showed that zebra mussels are destroying the food chain. They eat plants that were part of the diet of large fish like the lake trout. As a result, the lake trout must now eat large quantities of small fish that are high in mercury. Zebra mussels are an example of an invasive species, a species that is not native to the Great Lakes. Invasive species can harm the environment. They can also disrupt human activities, such as safely eating local fish.

2   The zebra mussels did not come here on their own. A ship first brought them in the 1980s by accident when it dumped wastewater in the Great Lakes. Zebra mussels found a perfect home in the Great Lakes. As they ate tiny plants, they took food away from native animals. This changed the ecosystem. As of 2019, people were still trying to find ways to control populations of zebra mussels in the Great Lakes.

3   Purple loosestrife is another invasive species. These purple flowering plants have tall spikes. They grow well in wetlands like those around the Great Lakes. Purple loosestrife spreads very easily. When it does, it takes space away from other native plants. The Great Lakes Aquatic Nonindigenous Species Information System (GLANSIS) reports that many native birds and moths do not seem to like living near this plant. All of this means that purple loosestrife is terrible for Great Lakes' wetlands. Nearby states are doing what they can to fight it. They are using beetles to lower plant numbers. They also warn visitors to clean seeds from their clothing, boats, and footwear.

4   In the above paragraphs, I only talked about two invasive species of the Great Lakes. But there are many more. New invasive species, such as Asian carp, threaten to cause new problems. But people have learned lessons from zebra mussels and purple loosestrife. They know action is needed. In 2020, government groups agreed to pay for protections to keep the new Asian carp invaders out of the Great Lakes. It is important to learn about invasive species so that we can all help protect our ecosystems.

FatCamera/E+/Getty Images

Paragraph 3

Reread the third paragraph. What is an example of a transitional word or phrase Sonya uses to connect her ideas?

_____

_____

_____

Underline an example of elaboration that Sonya uses. What does this elaboration support?

_____

_____

_____

_____

Paragraph 4

Reread the conclusion. **Circle** the sentence that restates Sonya's central idea from paragraph 1.

Apply the Rubric

With a partner, use the rubric on page 200 to discuss why Sonya scored a 4 on her essay.

Analyze the Prompt

Writing Prompt

Write an expository essay to present to your class about how plants, animals, and humans depend on each other to survive in their environment.

Purpose, Audience, and Task Reread the writing prompt. What is your purpose for writing? My purpose is to _____

_____

Who will your audience be? My audience will be _____

_____

What type of writing is the prompt asking for? _____

_____

Set a Purpose for Reading Sources Asking questions about what living things need to survive will help you figure out your purpose for reading. It will also help you understand what you already know about the topic. Before you read the passage set about ecology, write a question here.

_____

_____

_____

Life in Coral Reefs

1   Coral reefs are often called "the rain forests of the sea." Reefs have an abundance of life forms. **Many different animals find food and shelter in a coral reef.** A reef has a complex food web. Colorful fish, eels, octopuses, sponges, sharks, and sea turtles are some of the animals that call a reef home.

2   Reefs are made up of the hard shells of millions of corals. The hard shells of corals are called exoskeletons. As corals live and die, their exoskeletons create a giant, rocky honeycomb.

3   Living things in a coral reef depend on each other to survive. For example, corals and microscopic algae called zooxanthellae work together to build a reef.

4   Zooxanthellae live in the corals' soft tissue. There they are protected and get the sunlight they need to grow. In turn, the zooxanthellae provide the coral with oxygen and nutrients.

5   The zooxanthellae give the corals a rainbow of colors. When corals lose their zooxanthellae, they bleach, or turn white. And the corals will die unless the zooxanthellae are replaced. Scientists think that higher sea temperatures may be one reason why corals lose their color.

6   People around the world rely on reef fish and other animals for food. But in some places, people have overfished. People also use chemicals that pollute the ocean.

7   There has been a huge decline in the world's coral reefs since 1996. Today many reefs around the world are now protected areas. Scientists are trying to keep reefs healthy.

EXPOSITORY ESSAY

FIND TEXT EVIDENCE

Paragraph 1
Read the highlighted central idea in paragraph 1. **Circle** the sentence that uses examples to support the central idea.

Paragraphs 2–3
Underline the details that tell you what makes up a reef. What two living things work together to build a reef?

_____

_____

Paragraphs 4–5
Draw a box around what will happen if the zooxanthellae die and are not replaced.

Paragraphs 6–7
What may have caused the decline in coral reefs?

_____

_____

 Take Notes Paraphrase the central idea of the source and give examples of supporting details.

FIND TEXT EVIDENCE

Paragraphs 8–9

Read the highlighted detail in paragraph 9. How does this support the central idea?

_____

_____

Paragraphs 10–12

Circle the transition word in paragraph 11 that tells what happens if bees don't show up on farms where crops are grown.

How are people affected if honeybees don't pollinate?

_____

_____

_____

_____

Take Notes Paraphrase the central idea of the source and give examples of supporting details.

SOURCE 2

WHERE ARE THE BEES?

8   Beekeepers, researchers, and farmers want to know why millions of honeybees have disappeared since 2006. The bees left no clues.

9   Many states have spotted big problems with local bee colonies. A colony is a large group of bees that live and work together. Entire bee hives suddenly disappeared. **This has caused a decrease in honey production across the nation.**

10   Honeybees are hardworking insects. Not only do they make honey but they also help flowering plants grow. Bees move grains of pollen from one part of a flower to another, so a plant can grow seeds and fruit. This process is called pollination. Fruits and vegetables can't grow unless they're pollinated. Honeybees, birds, bats, and other insects are among nature's most important pollinators.

11   Honeybees pollinate about one third of the crops in the world. If honeybees don't pollinate, many crops won't produce fruit and seeds. Bees don't always show up on farms where crops are grown. Consequently, farmers rent colonies of bees to make sure their crops are pollinated. Beekeepers let the bees out to pollinate the crops. Then the bees return to their boxes, and they are moved to the next farm.

12   Experts meet to try to solve the mystery of the missing bees. A disease could be killing the bees. Hot, dry weather could be a cause. No one knows for sure, but many people are trying to help the bees survive.

Energy in the Everglades Ecosystem

13   Plants, animals, and water in the Everglades (a wetlands area in central and south Florida) form a remarkable ecosystem. There are a variety of birds, fish, mammals, reptiles, and amphibians (such as frogs and toads). Insect species number in the thousands. A variety of plants make their home in the Everglades, such as sawgrass, algae, mangroves, orchids, cypress trees, and wild flowers.

14   Look at the food web below. It shows how energy flows from the Sun through producers to consumers. Producers are organisms such as plants. They make their own food using sunlight. Consumers are organisms such as birds and mammals. They cannot make their own food and get energy from eating other organisms.

15   A food web is made up of many food chains. Energy passes from one organism to another in a food chain. All living things in the Everglades depend on one another to survive.

This food web represents only some of the animals and plants in an Everglades food web.

EXPOSITORY ESSAY

FIND TEXT EVIDENCE

Paragraph 13
Underline the things that make the Everglades a remarkable ecosystem.

Paragraphs 14–15
Draw a box around what a food web is made up of.

Circle the words that tell how energy passes through a food web.

Food Web Diagram
Describe one food chain you see in the food web.

_____

_____

_____

_____

_____

_____

_____

Take Notes Paraphrase the central idea of the source and give examples of supporting details.

WRITING

My Goal I can synthesize information from three sources.

TAKE NOTES

Read the writing prompt below. Then use the three sources, your notes, and the graphic organizer to plan a response.

Writing Prompt *Write an expository essay to present to your class about how plants, animals, and humans depend on each other to survive in their environment.*

✂ Synthesize Information

Review the evidence recorded from each source. How does the information show that living things need each other to survive in their environment? Discuss your ideas with a partner.

CHECK IN 1 2 3 4

Plan: Organize Ideas

Central Idea	Supporting Ideas
Plants, animals, and humans in the same ecosystem depend on each other for resources and protection.	Many living things survive together by trading resources.

Relevant Evidence

Source 1	Source 2	Source 3
Zooxanthellae live in coral where they're protected and get sunlight. Zooxanthellae give coral oxygen and nutrients. Coral dies without zooxanthellae.	Honeybees pollinate plants. They pollinate one third of the world's crops. Many of the plants we eat would not grow without honeybee pollination.	

Draft: Transitional Strategies

Connecting Ideas Transitional strategies include using transition words and phrases, also known as signal, or linking, words. Transition words and phrases help connect ideas in an essay. Organizational structures are also used to connect ideas. For example, in a cause-and-effect text structure, the cause tells why something happens and the effect tells what happens.

Words and phrases like *because, so, since, due to,* and *as a result* will help to signal cause-and-effect relationships.

Read the sentences below.

> Entire bee hives suddenly disappeared. This has caused a decrease in honey production across the nation.

Rewrite the above sentences. Use a transitional strategy to link the two ideas in the above sentences.

_____

_____

_____

 Draft Use your graphic organizer and examples above to write your draft in your writer's notebook. Before you start writing, review the rubric on page 200. Remember to vary your sentence lengths.

ToffeePhoto/Shutterstock

Grammar Connections

Possessive pronouns do not have an apostrophe because no letters are missing. *A honeycomb is made of wax cells. Its cells are shaped like hexagons.*

CHECK IN 1 2 3 4

Revise: Peer Conferences

Review a Draft Listen actively to your partner. Take notes about what you liked and what was difficult to follow. Begin by telling what you liked. Use these sentence starters.

I like the details you used to support the central idea because . . .
What did you mean by . . .
I think adding transitional words will help to . . . .

After you give each other feedback, reflect on the peer conference. How can you use the guidance from your partner to help improve your writing?

_____

_____

_____

Revision Use the Revising Checklist to help you figure out what text you may need to move, elaborate on, or delete. After you finish writing your final draft, use the full rubric on pages 240–243 to score your essay.

✓ Revising Checklist

☐ Does my essay present a strong central idea?

☐ Did I include enough relevant details to support my central idea?

☐ Did I use a variety of elaborative techniques?

☐ Did I use transitional strategies to show the connections between ideas?

☐ Did I check my spelling and punctuation?

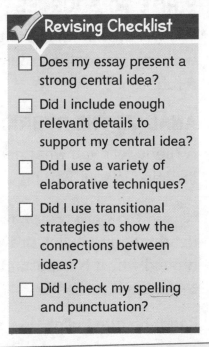

Next, you'll write an expository essay on a new topic.

My Score			
Purpose, Focus, & Organization (4 pts)	Evidence & Elaboration (4 pts)	Conventions (2 pts)	Total (10 pts)

WRITING

WRITE TO SOURCES

You will answer an expository writing prompt using sources and a rubric.

ANALYZE THE RUBRIC

A rubric tells you what needs to be included in your writing.

Purpose, Focus, and Organization

Read the third bullet. **Draw a box** around why it is important to use transitional strategies.

Read the fifth bullet. How should an expository essay end?

_____

Evidence and Elaboration

Read the fifth bullet. What is an example of a domain-specific word that you would use to write about a food web?

_____

_____

Read the sixth bullet. What is a synonym for the word *structure*?

_____

Expository Writing Rubric

Purpose, Focus, and Organization • Score 4
• stays focused on the purpose, audience, and task
• clearly presents and fully develops the central idea about a topic
• uses transitional strategies, such as words and phrases, to connect ideas
• uses a logical text structure to organize information
• **begins with a strong introduction and ends with a strong conclusion**

Evidence and Elaboration • Score 4
• effectively supports the central idea with convincing facts and details
• has strong examples of relevant evidence, or supporting details, from multiple sources
• uses elaborative techniques, such as facts, examples, definitions, and quotations from sources
• expresses interesting ideas clearly using precise language
• uses appropriate academic and domain-specific language
• uses different sentence structures

Turn to page 240 for the complete Expository Writing Rubric.

Strong Conclusion

Satisfying Endings A strong conclusion provides a satisfying ending to an essay. Your expository essay conclusion should restate the central idea, summarize the main points, and end with a final observation or thought.

Here is an example of a central idea in an introduction, or first paragraph. *Today the issues North Atlantic right whales face make them the world's most endangered large whale!*

Here is that central idea restated in the conclusion: *People need to do more to prevent the North Atlantic right whales from becoming extinct.*

Read the sentences below. They are part of an introduction. The central idea is highlighted.

> However, since 1970, North Atlantic right whales have been on the endangered species list. **Today the issues they face make them the world's most endangered large whale!**

Now you try it. Restate the highlighted central idea.

_____

_____

_____

Audience

Writers have an audience in mind when they write. They make choices about what to include based on their audience. Reread the paragraph about North Atlantic right whales. Who is the audience?

WRITING

ANALYZE THE STUDENT MODEL

Paragraph 1

Circle three different kinds of end punctuation in the first paragraph. What does using different end punctuation do?

_____

_____

_____

Paragraph 2

How does the information about why people hunted right whales in the past connect to the introduction?

_____

_____

_____

Draw a box around the transition words Jackie uses to connect why people liked hunting right whales to why so many were killed.

Student Model: Expository Essay

Jackie responded to the Writing Prompt: *Write an article for your school website about North Atlantic right whales and some of the issues that they face.* Read Jackie's essay below.

1   Have you ever seen a North Atlantic right whale? Unfortunately, odds are that you have not. According to the article "A Thousand Year Struggle for Survival," large numbers of these whales used to live in many parts of the Atlantic Ocean. However, since 1970, North Atlantic right whales have been on the endangered species list. Today the issues they face make them the world's most endangered large whale!

2   People have made survival difficult for the North Atlantic right whales for many years. They were hunted from the 800s on. Between 1600 and 1900, whalers killed about 5,500 right whales. There were only 100 left by 1930. In order to understand how this happened, it helps to know why people liked hunting them. These whales can grow to more than 50 feet long and weigh up to 70 tons. They were called "right whales" because they were slow, gentle, and easy to hunt. One whale meant a lot of food. It also had lots of oil that people could use for lamps.

3 Since the 1930s, rules had made it illegal to hunt North Atlantic right whales. Now these giants face new human-made problems. These whales live near the coasts of North America. Because they are so big, they can eat more than 2,000 pounds of tiny animals a day. In order to both find enough food and give birth in the right places, they migrate from north to south near the shore. According to "Facts About North Atlantic Right Whales," as the whales migrate, they cross through shipping lanes and fishing grounds. Boats can hit and kill them. They can get tangled in fishing gear. Underwater noise caused by human activities makes it hard for them to communicate with each other. Additionally, warming ocean waters are changing where the whales can find food. This forces the whales to change their movement patterns. They are going to new places without rules to protect the whales.

4 It is clear that people need to do more to prevent the North Atlantic right whales from becoming extinct. A group named Oceana decided to start a special campaign in 2019. They call the campaign "Right Whale to Save." Oceana teams are asking the United States and Canada to make better rules about fishing and boat speeds. Addressing these issues will help to further increase the number of North Atlantic right whales. That may allow them to survive into the future.

Africa Studio/Shutterstock

Paragraph 3

Reread the third paragraph. **Underline** the dangers faced by North Atlantic right whales. Give an example of relevant evidence that Jackie uses to support the idea that North Atlantic right whales are in danger.

_____

_____

Circle an example of elaboration that Jackie uses to explain why changing movement patterns can be dangerous.

Paragraph 4

Reread the fourth paragraph. **Draw a box** around the idea that Jackie restates from paragraph 1.

Apply the Rubric

With a partner, use the rubric on page 212 to discuss why Jackie scored a 4 on his essay.

Analyze the Prompt

Writing Prompt

Write an expository essay for a school magazine about how writers were inspired by special places.

Purpose, Audience, and Task Reread the writing prompt. What is your purpose for writing? My purpose is to _____

_____

Who will your audience be? My audience will be _____

_____

What type of writing is the prompt asking for? _____

_____

Set a Purpose for Reading Sources Asking questions about how places inspire writers will help you figure out your purpose for reading. It will also help you understand what you already know about the topic. Before you read the passage set about authors who wrote about special places, write a question here.

_____

_____

_____

Read the following passage set.

A Fight to Truly Be Heard

1   Sometimes sharing a love of place can be difficult. This was true for a Native American woman who grew up among Washington's Confederated Colville Tribes. She was born Christine Quintasket, but chose the name Mourning Dove as a writer. She wanted to stand up for inaccurate images of her people. In her day, that was not easy.

2   Mourning Dove's life began in what is now Washington State on the Colville Reservation. Her mother was a Colville tribal member; her father was of the Okanogan tribe. Mourning Dove spent early days on the Columbia River, learning traditional lifeways from her grandmother. As a little girl she loved joining in the great salmon harvest at Kettle Falls.

Upper Columbia River

3   With her grandmother in 1908, Mourning Dove saw the last roundup of free ranging bison. "One magnificent fellow," she later said, "fought like a lion." As the years passed, this event stayed deep in her heart. It inspired her to write a novel. A white businessman named Lucullus Virgil McWhorter offered to help her. Unfortunately, his help changed the writing completely. Mourning Dove herself wrote, "I feel like it was someone else's book and not mine at all." Mourning Dove later wrote *Coyote Stories,* a book of traditional Pacific Northwest stories. Again, others edited and changed her writing.

4   After Mourning Dove's death, people found she had left behind many writings. Those writings became her autobiography, her own story of her life. Today, many honor her as an important historical Native voice.

AlpamayoPhoto/E+/Getty Images

EXPOSITORY ESSAY

FIND TEXT EVIDENCE

Paragraph 1
Underline the central idea in the first paragraph.

Paragraph 2
Draw a box around one of the details that describes traditional lifeways.

Paragraph 3
Circle the sentences that tell what event stayed deep within Mourning Dove's heart. What did this inspire her to do?

_____

_____

Paragraph 4
After Mourning Dove's death, what type of writing came from the work she left behind?

Take Notes Paraphrase how Mourning Dove felt about what others did to her writing and include some of her own words in your notes.

Unit 2 · Expository Writing   217

Paragraph 5

Underline the words that tell you how White and his wife felt about New York City. How is the farm described?

_____

_____

Paragraphs 6–8

Circle the details that tell you where White loved to spend his time.

How did studying a real-life spider inspire White?

_____

_____

_____

Read the highlighted conclusion. **Draw a box around** a detail that tells you why White celebrated animals in his writing.

Take Notes Paraphrase the central idea of the source and give examples of supporting details.

SOURCE 2

Inspiration on a Farm

5   E.B. White and his wife lived in New York City, but were not happy with city life. After spying a beautiful old Maine farm while on a sailing trip, they decided to buy it. This move to the country eventually gave White the inspiration for his most famous book, *Charlotte's Web*.

6   White grew up in Mount Vernon, New York. There he loved to spend time in a large stable filled with animals. The farm White bought as an adult reminded him of those quiet, thoughtful days. "When I got a place in the country," White wrote, "I was quite sure animals would appear, and they did."

7   One day, White became curious about a spider who was spinning a web in his barn. White decided to learn more about that species. He began to imagine a spider writing letters on her web. His research and real-life observations mixed in his imagination. These ideas led to one of the most beloved children's books of all time. White's barn and its animals are at the center of *Charlotte's Web*.

8   White had always felt shy in public. But he felt comfortable with animals. It makes sense that his most famous book celebrates his barn full of animals. **White's love of farm life shines through in** *Charlotte's Web*.

E.B. White's house was a farm in Brooklin, Maine. It is also known as The House at Allen Cove.

Fred Field/Portland Press Herald/Getty Images

A Writer to Celebrate

9   Zora Neale Hurston, a famous American writer, lived in and traveled to many places. However, the town of Eatonville, Florida, always held a special place in her heart. Eatonville is important in American history as it was the first US city established by free African Americans, in 1887. Hurston wrote that in that town "the air is sweet, yes, literally sweet." Hurston was born in Alabama in 1891. Her family moved to Eatonville a year later. More than any other place, Eatonville and the wilderness just outside of it inspired her.

10   The people Hurston met, the stories she heard, and Eatonville's natural surroundings influenced her writing. In one book, Hurston wrote, "the mocking birds sang all night and alligators trumpeted from their stronghold." When describing a return to Eatonville, she wrote, "The curtain of trees along the river shut out the world. . . . The smothering foliage that draped riverbanks, the miles of purple hyacinths, all thrilled me anew."

11   Hurston left Florida as a young woman. She studied at Howard University in Washington, D.C., Barnard College in New York City, and did graduate work at Columbia University. She studied anthropology, the study of cultures. Hurston focused on African American culture. She was an accomplished writer of plays, novels, and stories.

12   Hurston returned to Central Florida later in life. During her last years, she lived in the city of Fort Pierce. People in Eatonville and Fort Pierce continue to honor Hurston. They lovingly remember a writer who celebrated their communities.

EXPOSITORY ESSAY

FIND TEXT EVIDENCE

Paragraph 9
Underline the details that tell what inspired Hurston.

Paragraph 10
Circle the details that tell what influenced Hurston's writing. What is one example of how Hurston described her surroundings?

_____

_____

_____

Paragraphs 11–12
Draw a box around the types of Hurston's writings. How do the people of Eatonville and Fort Pierce feel about Hurston?

_____

_____

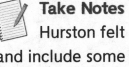

Take Notes Paraphrase how Hurston felt about Florida and include some of her own words in your notes.

WRITING

TAKE NOTES

Read the writing prompt below. Then use the three sources, your notes, and the graphic organizer to plan a response.

Writing Prompt *Write an expository essay for a school magazine about how writers were inspired by special places.*

Synthesize Information

Review your notes and the evidence in your graphic organizer. What is it about certain special places that helped to inspire these three famous writers? Discuss your ideas with a partner.

Plan: Organize Ideas

Central Idea	Supporting Ideas
Special places can inspire writers.	Three famous writers found inspiration at special places.

CHECK IN 1 2 3 4

Relevant Evidence		
Source 1	**Source 2**	**Source 3**
Mourning Dove spent early days following traditions on a reservation.	White found inspiration on a farm observing animals.	The towns where Hurston settled honor her for celebrating their communities.

Draft: Relevant Evidence

Relevant Evidence Writers use relevant evidence, or supporting details, from multiple sources to support their central ideas. Relevant evidence may include important facts, details, examples, or quotations. Read a draft of a paragraph from page 215 that Jackie wrote. Underline the central idea.

> Since the 1930s, rules had made it illegal to hunt North Atlantic right whales. Now these giants face new human-made problems. These whales live near the coasts of North America. Because they are so big, they can eat more than 2,000 pounds of tiny animals a day. They use special plates called baleen to sift out their food. In order to both find enough food and give birth in the right places, they migrate from north to south near the shore.

Cross out the sentence that is not relevant and does not support the central idea. What does the rest of the evidence give information about?

_____

_____

_____

_____

_____

 Draft Use your graphic organizer and notes to write your draft in your writer's notebook. Before you start writing, review the rubric on page 212. Remember to indent each paragraph.

C Squared Studios/Photodisc/Getty Images

Grammar Connections

Remember to capitalize the first, last, and all main words in the title of a book. Conjunctions, articles (*a, an, the*), and short prepositions are not capitalized. In the book title *The Old Man and the Sea*, "The" is capitalized because it is the first word in the title.

CHECK IN 1 2 3 4

Revise: Peer Conferences

COLLABORATE

Review a Draft Listen actively to your partner. Take notes about what you liked and what was difficult to follow. Begin by telling what you liked. Use these sentence starters.

I like the evidence you used to support the central idea because . . .
Your transitional words helped me understand . . .
What did you mean by . . .

After you give each other feedback, reflect on the peer conference. How can you use the guidance from your partner to help improve your writing?

_____

_____

_____

Revision Use the Revising Checklist to help you figure out what text you may need to move, elaborate on, or delete. After you finish writing your final draft, use the full rubric on pages 240–243 to score your essay.

Turn to page 199. Fill in the bars to show what you learned.

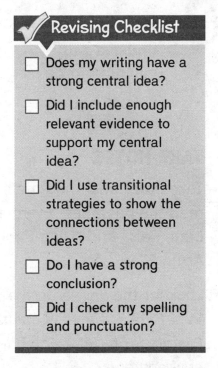

✔ Revising Checklist

- ☐ Does my writing have a strong central idea?
- ☐ Did I include enough relevant evidence to support my central idea?
- ☐ Did I use transitional strategies to show the connections between ideas?
- ☐ Do I have a strong conclusion?
- ☐ Did I check my spelling and punctuation?

My Score			
Purpose, Focus, & Organization (4 pts)	Evidence & Elaboration (4 pts)	Conventions (2 pts)	Total (10 pts)

TAKE NOTES

Take notes and annotate as you read the passages "Everglades Mammals" and "Nine-Banded Armadillos."

Look for the answer to the question: *What are some ways animals in the Everglades have adapted to their environments?*

_____

_____

_____

_____

_____

_____

_____

_____

_____

PASSAGE 1

EXPOSITORY TEXT

Everglades Mammals

More than forty native species of mammals live in the Everglades. These mammals include rabbits, deer, gray foxes, manatees, and panthers. Some of these animals have unique characteristics and behaviors.

Marsh rabbits have adapted to their watery environment by learning to swim! No other rabbits are known to be swimmers. These rabbits live in freshwater marshes, pinelands, and coastal prairies. They eat a variety of plants and are active at night.

Gray foxes are the only foxes that have learned to climb trees. These unique animals are flexible eaters. Although they eat mainly rabbits and rodents, they also eat birds, insects, acorns, and fruit.

White-tailed deer are found in many parts of North America and South America. They have white on their tails and brown hides. The Everglades white-tailed deer are smaller than other white-tailed deer. Because they live in a warm climate, they lack a layer of fat that other white-tailed deer have. These plant eaters spend most of their time feeding in the sawgrass marshes and prairies.

West Indian manatees live in the coastal areas. They can weigh up to 1,200 pounds and grow between 8 and 13 feet long. They like to munch on sea grasses and foliage, and can spend 6 to 8 hours each day eating.

marsh rabbit

gray fox

white-tailed deer

West Indian manatee

Florida **panthers** are very similar to other panthers found in other parts of North America. They are active at night and stay out of sight. But they are also a bit different. Florida panthers are smaller and have a head that is shaped differently than other panthers' heads. Scientists believe the shape of their head is an adaptation to the humid Everglades environment. Panthers are at the top of the Everglades food chain. Their favorite foods are white-tailed deer and wild hogs, but they also eat rabbits, raccoons, birds, and other smaller animals.

panther

PASSAGE 2

EXPOSITORY TEXT

Nine-Banded Armadillos

In Spanish, *armadillo* means "little armored one." The armadillo is the only living mammal that has this unique protection. Armadillos are relatives of anteaters and sloths. Despite its name, the nine-banded armadillo can have between seven and eleven bands.

An average armadillo is about 2.5 feet long and weighs about 12 pounds. In the wild, armadillos live between 7 and 20 years. They do not have a lot of body fat. Therefore, they like warm climates. They live in a variety of environments including rain forests, grasslands, and semi-deserts. There are twenty species of armadillo. The nine-banded armadillo is the only one found in the United States. They primarily reside in south-central states. However, they have been found as far east as North Carolina and as far north as Illinois.

TAKE NOTES

TAKE NOTES

Armadillos have certain traits that are inherited and some that are learned. For example, armadillos inherit, or are born with, pointy snouts. With their pointy snouts, armadillos can find almost 500 different foods! Armadillos are omnivores, which means they eat animals and plants. They have poor eyesight, so they rely on their keen sense of smell. Much of their diet consists of insects. They eat some fruit, seeds, and fungi.

A behavior that armadillos learn is to look for food in the early morning and evening when their enemies are sleeping. Their enemies include dogs, alligators, coyotes, and humans. When startled, a nine-banded armadillo can jump up about 3 to 4 feet into the air before it starts to run.

These animals could be called antisocial because they like to be alone. In fact, armadillos spend most of their time sleeping. They do get together to mate and to keep warm. Despite their armor, they aren't afraid of the water. By inflating their stomachs, armadillos can float. Some have been known to hold their breath for 6 minutes or more.

(bkg) Joesboy/iStock/Getty Images

COMPARE THE PASSAGES

Create a Venn diagram like the one below. Use your notes and the diagram to show how one of the mammals in "Everglades Mammals" is alike and different from the armadillo described in "Nine-Banded Armadillos." Fill in the name of the mammal you choose on the line in the left oval.

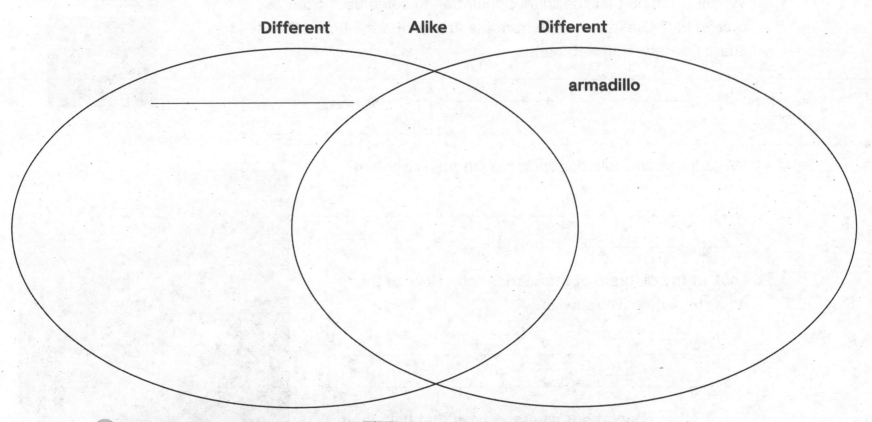

Different   **Alike**   **Different**

armadillo

Synthesize Information

Think about all you have learned about adaptation in this unit. What questions do you have about animal adaptations? What else would you like to learn about animal adaptations? Write your response in your reader's notebook.

SHARKS UNDER ATTACK

COLLABORATE

Log on to **my.mheducation.com** and reread the online *Time for Kids* article "Sharks Under Attack." Pay attention to the information found in the interactive elements. Answer the questions below.

Sharks Under Attack

Shark populations around the world are shrinking. Steps are being taken to save the fish before it's too late.

Time for Kids: "Sharks Under Attack"

- Why is it difficult for the shark population to come back from overfishing? Use information from the article and the linked Global Shark Conservation web page.

_____

_____

- What important role do sharks play in the ecosystem?

_____

_____

- Look at the diagram of the shark's body. How do the fins on a shark help it to survive?

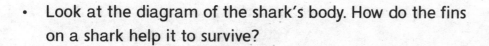

_____

_____

- What other adaptations do sharks have that help them survive?

_____

_____

tswinner/iStock/Getty Images

CREATE A PODCAST

Use the information from your Venn diagram on page 227 to create a podcast about the similarities and differences between the mammal you chose and the armadillo.

I chose to compare armadillos to _____ because

_____

_____

_____

_____

The mammals are alike because

_____

_____

_____

The mammals are different because

_____

_____

_____

I can read and understand social studies texts.

TAKE NOTES

Take notes and annotate as you read the passages "Volunteering at National Parks" and "A Hero of Conservation."

Look for the answer to the question: *What are some ways volunteers can protect plants and animals?*

_____

_____

_____

_____

_____

_____

_____

_____

_____

_____

PASSAGE 1

EXPOSITORY TEXT

Volunteering at National Parks

National parks welcome volunteers of all ages. It takes a lot of hard work to maintain and preserve the natural beauty of our parks.

The Volunteers-In-Parks program with the National Park Service offers short, one-time volunteer roles, as well as positions that last several days. Volunteer roles can be in front of the public or behind the scenes. Hundreds of volunteer positions exist across the United States. From digging for fossils to underwater diving to history reenactments, volunteers make a big difference in the national parks.

Some national parks have research learning centers. These centers provide opportunities for people to participate in collecting scientific data. This activity has become popular and is called "citizen science." Citizen scientists learn how to maintain an ecosystem.

One organization that partners with the National Park Service is called the Community Volunteer Ambassadors (CVA). CVA is a youth organization made of recent high school and college graduates. The goal of the organization is to help form bonds between communities and the national parks. CVA helps to connect schools, businesses, and clubs that are looking for volunteer opportunities with the National Park Service. Park supervisors train the volunteers. One of CVA's goals is to increase the number of volunteers at parks.

Kitty May/DorkyPix

The types of national park sites are quite diverse. In addition to natural parks, the system includes battlefields, historical parks, lakeshores, national monuments, parkways, scenic trails, and many others. Volunteers play an active role within all types of national parks. Many offer jobs that help plants and animals. If a volunteer likes dogs, he or she may want to be a Bark Ranger. Bark Rangers are volunteers who educate the public about the park's pet policies and pet safety. Some parks offer volunteers a chance to work in natural animal habitats to study and report on rare and endangered species, such as sea turtles. All of the volunteer roles are very important jobs.

If you are interested in learning more about volunteering, go to the National Park Service (NPS) website. There you will find information about opportunities for volunteers. With your class or with family members, you can explore the wonders of nature while giving a helping hand.

PASSAGE 2

BIOGRAPHY

A Hero of **Conservation**

Mabel Rosalie Barrow, called Rosalie, was born in 1877 to a wealthy New York family. When traveling to England as a young woman, she met Charles Noel Edge. They married in 1909, and she became Rosalie Barrow Edge. The couple traveled to Europe often, but their home was in New York. One of Edge's trips to Europe played a significant role in her life.

TAKE NOTES

TAKE NOTES

_____

_____

_____

_____

_____

_____

_____

_____

_____

_____

_____

_____

_____

_____

_____

_____

While in England, Edge met Margaret Thomas, a women's suffragist. A suffragist is someone who advocates for the equal rights of women. Thomas inspired Edge, and Edge was ready to join the suffragist movement in America. Her work as a suffragist helped lead to the passage of the Nineteenth Amendment in 1920, giving American women the right to vote. Through her experiences as a suffragist, Edge learned the power of communicating well-crafted ideas. She was determined and ready to stand up for her beliefs.

Edge had a passion for bird watching. In 1929, she learned that some nature conservation groups were making money in ways that hurt wild creatures. Edge was furious. From her experience as a suffragist, she knew she had the ability to make a change and make a difference. She started the Environmental Conservation Committee. The ECC exposed the corruption and sought reform. In the 1930s, Edge helped to create the first sanctuary for birds of prey near Kempton, Pennsylvania. Today it is called Hawk Mountain Sanctuary. Her conservation efforts also led to the founding of two national parks and to increased environmental protections at other national parks and sites.

For the rest of her life, Edge never gave up pushing others to do better in protecting wild animals and places. She was known to be determined, honest, and one of the greatest conservationists of her time. Edge's activism inspired many others and helped to shape modern American nature conservation.

COMPARE THE PASSAGES

Review your notes from both passages. Then create a Venn diagram like the one below. Use your notes and the diagram to record how the information in the two passages is alike and different.

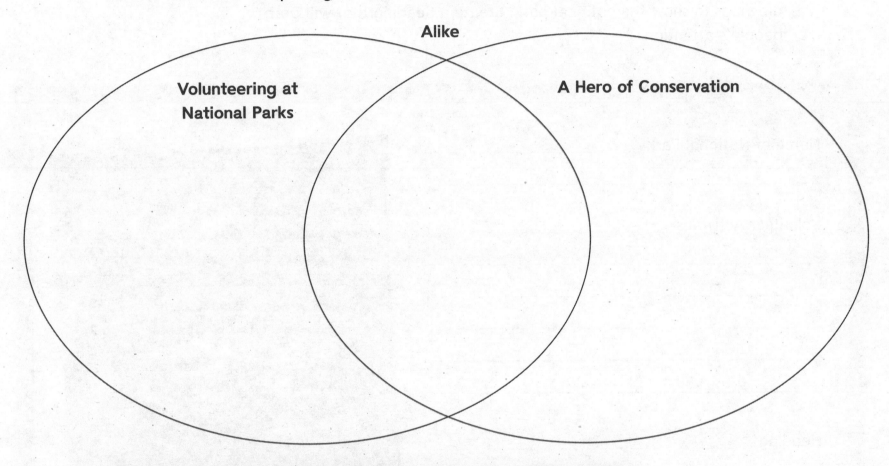

Alike

Volunteering at
National Parks

A Hero of Conservation

Synthesize Information

Think about both passages you read. Why are public service, conservation, community involvement, and volunteering so important? Write your response in your reader's notebook.

CHECK IN 1 2 3 4

MAKE A VOLUNTEER POSTER

Make a poster to encourage people to volunteer at a national park. Choose a national park. Research volunteer opportunities available at the park. Describe a few activities that are needed. Use photographs or drawings to show the national park. Create a heading that will grab people's attention.

Name of National Park _____

_____

Volunteer Activities _____

_____

_____

_____

_____

Heading _____

_____

Reflect on Your Learning

Talk About It Reflect on what you learned in this unit. Then talk with a partner about how you did.

I am really proud of how I can _____

_____

_____

_____

_____

Something I need to work more on is _____

_____

_____

_____

_____

My Goal Set a goal for Unit 3. In your reader's notebook, write about what you can do to get there.

Share a goal you have with a partner.

Argumentative Writing Rubric

Score	Purpose, Focus, and Organization (4-point Rubric)	Evidence and Elaboration (4-point Rubric)	Conventions of Standard English (2-point Rubric begins at score point 2)
4	• stays focused on the purpose, audience, and task • makes a claim that clearly supports a perspective • uses transitional strategies, such as words and phrases, to connect ideas • presents ideas in a logical progression, or order • begins with a strong introduction and ends with a strong conclusion	• effectively supports the claim with logical reasons • has strong examples of relevant evidence, or supporting details, from multiple sources • uses elaborative techniques, such as examples, definitions, and quotations from sources • expresses interesting ideas clearly using precise language • uses appropriate academic and domain-specific language • uses different sentence structures	

Score	Purpose, Focus, and Organization (4-point Rubric)	Evidence and Elaboration (4-point Rubric)	Conventions of Standard English (2-point Rubric begins at score point 2)
3	• generally stays focused on the purpose, audience, and task • makes a claim that mostly supports a perspective • uses some transitional strategies, such as words and phrases, to connect ideas • presents ideas in a mostly logical progression, or order • begins with an acceptable introduction and ends with a sufficient conclusion	• mostly supports the claim with some logical reasons • has some examples of mostly relevant evidence, or supporting details, from multiple sources • uses some elaborative techniques, such as examples, definitions, and quotations from sources • generally expresses interesting ideas using both precise and general language • mostly uses appropriate academic and domain-specific language • mostly uses different sentence structures	

Argumentative Writing Rubric

Score	Purpose, Focus, and Organization (4-point Rubric)	Evidence and Elaboration (4-point Rubric)	Conventions of Standard English (2-point Rubric)
2	• stays somewhat focused on the purpose, audience, and task, but may include unimportant details • does not make a clear claim or does not completely support a perspective • uses few transitional strategies to connect ideas • may present ideas that do not follow a logical progression, or order • may begin with an inadequate introduction or end with an unsatisfactory conclusion	• shows some support of the claim with logical reasons • has weak and inappropriate examples of evidence or does not include enough sources • may not use elaborative techniques effectively • expresses some interesting ideas, but ideas are simple and vague • uses limited academic and domain-specific language • may use only simple sentence structures	• has a sufficient command of grammar and usage • has a sufficient command of capitalization, punctuation, spelling, and sentence formation • has slight errors in grammar and usage that do not affect meaning

(bkgd) Valentain Jevee/Shutterstock

Score	Purpose, Focus, and Organization (4-point Rubric)	Evidence and Elaboration (4-point Rubric)	Conventions of Standard English (2-point Rubric)
1	• is not aware of the purpose, audience, and task • does not make a claim or does not support a perspective • uses few or no transitional strategies to connect ideas • does not present ideas in a logical progression, or order • does not include an introduction nor a conclusion	• supports the claim with few logical reasons or does not support the claim at all • has few or no examples of evidence or does not include enough sources • does not use elaborative techniques • has confusing or unclear ideas or does not express any interesting ideas • does not demonstrate a grasp of academic and domain-specific language • consists only of simple sentence structures	• has an incomplete command of grammar and usage • has an incomplete command of capitalization, punctuation, spelling, and sentence formation • has some errors in grammar and usage that may affect meaning
0			• does not have a command of grammar and usage • does not have a command of capitalization, punctuation, spelling, and sentence formation • has too many serious errors in grammar and usage that frequently disrupt meaning

Expository Writing Rubric

Score	Purpose, Focus, and Organization (4-point Rubric)	Evidence and Elaboration (4-point Rubric)	Conventions of Standard English (2-point Rubric begins at score point 2)
4	• stays focused on the purpose, audience, and task • clearly presents and fully develops the central idea about a topic • uses transitional strategies, such as words and phrases, to connect ideas • uses a logical text structure to organize information • begins with a strong introduction and ends with a strong conclusion	• effectively supports the central idea with convincing facts and details • has strong examples of relevant evidence, or supporting details, from multiple sources • uses elaborative techniques, such as facts, examples, definitions, and quotations from sources • expresses interesting ideas clearly using precise language • uses appropriate academic and domain-specific language • uses different sentence structures	

Score	Purpose, Focus, and Organization (4-point Rubric)	Evidence and Elaboration (4-point Rubric)	Conventions of Standard English (2-point Rubric begins at score point 2)
3	<ul><li>generally stays focused on the purpose, audience, and task</li><li>presents and develops the central idea about a topic in a mostly clear and complete way, although there may be some unimportant details</li><li>uses some transitional strategies, such as words and phrases, to connect ideas</li><li>uses a mostly logical text structure to organize information</li><li>begins with an acceptable introduction and ends with a sufficient conclusion</li></ul>	<ul><li>mostly supports the central idea with some convincing facts and details</li><li>has some examples of mostly relevant evidence, or supporting details, from multiple sources</li><li>uses some elaborative techniques, such as facts, examples, definitions, and quotations from sources</li><li>generally expresses interesting ideas using both precise and general language</li><li>mostly uses appropriate academic and domain-specific language</li><li>mostly uses different sentence structures</li></ul>	

Expository Writing Rubric

Score	Purpose, Focus, and Organization (4-point Rubric)	Evidence and Elaboration (4-point Rubric)	Conventions of Standard English (2-point Rubric)
2	• stays somewhat focused on the purpose, audience, and task, but may include unimportant details • does not clearly present or develop a central idea • uses few transitional strategies to connect ideas • may not follow a logical text structure to organize information • may begin with an inadequate introduction or end with an unsatisfactory conclusion	• shows some support of the central idea with few convincing facts and details • has weak and inappropriate examples of evidence or does not include enough sources • may not use elaborative techniques effectively • expresses some interesting ideas, but ideas are simple and vague • uses limited academic and domain-specific language • may use only simple sentence structures	• has a sufficient command of grammar and usage • has a sufficient command of capitalization, punctuation, spelling, and sentence formation • has slight errors in grammar and usage that do not affect meaning

Score	Purpose, Focus, and Organization (4-point Rubric)	Evidence and Elaboration (4-point Rubric)	Conventions of Standard English (2-point Rubric)
1	• is not aware of the purpose, audience, and task • does not have a central idea • uses few or no transitional strategies to connect ideas • does not follow a logical text structure to organize information • does not include an introduction nor a conclusion	• supports the central idea with few facts and details or does not support the central idea at all • has few or no examples of evidence or does not include enough sources • does not use elaborative techniques • has confusing or unclear ideas or does not express any interesting ideas • does not demonstrate a grasp of academic and domain-specific language • consists only of simple sentence structures	• has an incomplete command of grammar and usage • has an incomplete command of capitalization, punctuation, spelling, and sentence formation • has some errors in grammar and usage that may affect meaning
0			• does not have a command of grammar and usage • does not have a command of capitalization, punctuation, spelling, and sentence formation • has too many serious errors in grammar and usage that frequently disrupt meaning